Morals and Manners in Islam

A Guide to Islamic Ādāb

MARWĀN IBRĀHĪM AL-KAYSĪ

The Islamic Foundation

© The Islamic Foundation 1986/1406 AH. Reprinted 1989/1409 AH

ISBN 0 86037 167 0 (HB)
ISBN 0 86037 168 9 (PB)

All rights reserved. No part of this publication may be reproduced, stored in a retrieval system, or transmitted in any form or by any means, electronic, mechanical, photocopying, recording or otherwise, without the prior permission of the copyright owner.

Published by
The Islamic Foundation
223 London Road
Leicester LE2 1ZE, United Kingdom

British Library Cataloguing in Publication Data
Al-Kaysī, Marwān Ibrāhīm
  Morals and manners in Islam: a guide
  to Islamic Ādāb.
  1. Religious life (Islam)
  I. Title
  297'.44   BP188

ISBN 0-86037-167-0
ISBN 0-86037-168-9 Pbk

Printed in Great Britain by Dotesios Printers Ltd, Trowbridge, Wiltshire

To

my unforgettable daughters

A'isha and 'Ula

whose love and affection have so influenced my life

Contents

Preface 11

Chapter 1: Introduction 13
Sources 13; Characteristics: Comprehensiveness and Morality 16; Goals 20; Kindness and Gentleness 23; Consideration For Others 24; Role of *Ādāb al-Islām* in Social Relationships 25; Religious Aspect of *Ādāb al-Islām* 28; Psychological Aspect of *Ādāb al-Islām* 31; Medical and Hygienic Aspects of *Ādāb al-Islām* 31; Contribution of *Ādāb al-Islām* to the National Economy 35; Marriage, the Family and *Ādāb al-Islām* 36; Norms of Sexual Behaviour in Islam 40; *Ādāb al-Islām* and the Status of Women 42; *Ādāb al-Islām* and Discipline 44; Concern About Human Safety 45; *Ādāb al-Islām* for the Preservation of Unity and the Cultural Identity of Muslims 46; Islamic Attitude Toward Manners and Customs of Non-Muslims 48; Overview of the Principal Rules of Islamic Conduct 49

Chapter 2: Bodily Functions 55
Sneezing 55; Yawning 56; Going to Bed 57; Relieving Oneself 60; Menstruation and Child-Bed 62; Man's Seminally Defiled State 63

Chapter 3: Cleanliness and Purity 65
    Impurities 65; Bathing 65; Cosmetics and Adornment for Men 68; Women's Make-Up and Adornment 70; General Guidelines for Both Sexes 71

Chapter 4: Table Manners 73
    The Meal 73; Sitting Down to Eat 74; Proper Table Manners 74; Drinking 77

Chapter 5: Dress 81
    Common Principles 81; Men's Dress 82; Women's Dress 83; Shoes 85

Chapter 6: Architecture and Furniture 87
    The Muslim Dwelling 87; Precautionary Measures For Safety at Home 89

Chapter 7: Conduct Within the Family 91
    Husband-Wife Relationship 91; Correct Conduct of a Muslim Wife 94; Parents' Conduct Toward Their Children 96; Children's Conduct Toward Their Parents 99

Chapter 8: Reading and Reciting the Qur'ān 103

Chapter 9: The Mosque 107
    Design 107; Cleanliness and Tidiness 108

Chapter 10: Behaviour on Fridays 109
    Khuṭbah at Friday Prayer 111

Chapter 11: Celebrating the Feasts 113
    Observing the Feasts 113; Behaviour on *'Īd al-Aḍḥā* 115; Special Instructions for *'Īd al-Fiṭr* 116

Chapter 12: Marriage 117
    The Search For a Wife 117; The Woman's Right and Responsibility in Choosing a Husband 119; The Engagement 119; The Marriage Contract 120; The Wedding Party 121; Conjugal Relations 121; Advice for Men 122; Advice for Women 123; The Wedding Feast 123; Polygamy 124

Chapter 13: Births 127
The Announcement 127; Congratulations and Visits 128; Seventh-Day Celebration 128; Circumcision Ceremony 129

Chapter 14: Giving Names and Addressing Others 131
Giving Names 131; Addressing Others 132

Chapter 15: Social Life 135
Good Social Relations 135; Talking and Listening 141; Language Preferred in Speech 142; Listening 145; Swearing 145; *Nadhr* 146; Laughter 147; Weeping 147; Jokes 148; Behaviour When Meeting Others 148; Manners of Greeting 150; Asking Permission to Enter Another's House 153; At a Friend's House 154; Receiving Guests 156; Inviting Others to Dine 157; When Invited to a Meal 158; Visiting the Sick 159; Group Meetings 160; Forms of Sitting 163; Women's Conduct Outside the Home 163; Celebrations 164; Behaviour Toward Relatives 165; Behaviour Toward Neighbours 166; Gifts 167

Chapter 16: Behaviour in Various Situations 169
In the Mosque 169; At the Cemetery 171; On the Street 172

Chapter 17: Funerals 175
Things That Need to be Done When Someone Dies 175; Escorting the Funeral 176; Burial 178; After the Burial 179; Condolences 180; Mourning 181

Chapter 18: Cemetery Architecture 183
Location 183; Interior Grave Design 183; Exterior Grave Design 184

Chapter 19: Travelling 185

Chapter 20: Sports 191

Chapter 21: Treatment of Animals 193

Bibliography 196

Index 197

TRANSLITERATION OF ARABIC WORDS AND NAMES

ا ،	consonantal sound	a	ط	....	ṭ
ا	long vowel	ā	ظ	....	ẓ
ب	....	b	ع	....	' inverted apostrophe
ت	....	t	غ	....	gh
ث	....	th	ف	....	f
ج	....	j	ق	....	q
ح	....	ḥ	ك	....	k
خ	....	kh	ل	....	l
د	....	d	م	....	m
ذ	....	dh	ن	....	n
ر	....	r	ه	....	h
ز	....	z	و	consonant	w
س	....	s	و	long vowel	ū
ش	....	sh	و	dipthong	au
ص	....	ṣ	ى	consonant	y
ض	....	ḍ	ى	long vowel	ī
			ى	dipthong	ai

8

بِسْمِ اللّهِ الرَّحْمنِ الرَّحِيمِ

ان الحمد لله نحمده ونستعينه ونستغفره، ونعوذ بالله من شرور انفسنا ومن سيئات اعمالنا، من يهده الله فلا مضل له، ومن يضلل فلا هادي له، وأشهد ان لا إله إلا الله وحده لا شريك له، وأشهد أن محمدا عبده ورسوله.

﴿يَاأَيُّهَا الَّذِينَ آمَنُوا اتَّقُوا اللهَ حَقَّ تُقَاتِهِ وَلَا تَمُوتُنَّ إِلَّا وَأَنْتُمْ مُسْلِمُونَ﴾

﴿يَاأَيُّهَا النَّاسُ اتَّقُوا رَبَّكُمُ الَّذِي خَلَقَكُمْ مِنْ نَفْسٍ وَاحِدَةٍ وَخَلَقَ مِنْهَا زَوْجَهَا، وَبَثَّ مِنْهُمَا رِجَالًا كَثِيرًا وَنِسَاءً، وَاتَّقُوا اللهَ الَّذِي تَسَاءَلُونَ بِهِ وَالأَرْحَامَ، إِنَّ اللهَ كَانَ عَلَيْكُمْ رَقِيبًا﴾

﴿يَاأَيُّهَا الَّذِينَ آمَنُوا اتَّقُوا اللهَ وَقُولُوا قَوْلًا سَدِيدًا يُصْلِحْ لَكُمْ أَعْمَالَكُمْ وَيَغْفِرْ لَكُمْ ذُنُوبَكُمْ، وَمَنْ يُطِعِ اللهَ وَرَسُولَهُ فَقَدْ فَازَ فَوْزًا عَظِيمًا﴾

Preface

Since the beginning of history, human societies, even primitive tribal communities, have all developed rules to regulate the conduct of personal and social relations. The oldest book on manners, *The Instructions of Ptah Hotep*, attributed to the ancient Egyptians, records the instructions of a father to his son about proper behaviour. Every people has observed its own rules and norms; manners have changed tremendously over the centuries, indeed, even within a single people they have varied considerably from one place to another at one and the same time. Regarding Muslims, it is true that many elements of Islamic manners still dominate different spheres of daily life in the Muslim world. Nevertheless, it is also true that alien elements have had a wide and increasing influence. This is due primarily to a weak interaction with the Islamic faith. But the fact that no standard text on the subject exists has also contributed. This work is a response to the need for such a text, making the details of Islamic manners readily accessible to the largest possible audience.

The importation of certain elements of Western manners into the Muslim's daily life has come out of the recent and continuing interaction with the West. But even before that interaction had been established, the Islamic way of life had been subject to non-Islamic elements, chiefly the result of innovation. To meet this challenge, a Muslim must Islamize his conception of manners by deriving them from the basic sources of Islam, the Qur'ān and the *Sunnah*. He must distinguish between normative Islam and historical Islam, between Islam and non-Islam; he must point to many practices which, ungrounded in normative Islam, yet prevail among Muslims. Having done this, the way ahead will be clearer for Islamic communities to rid themselves of cultural influences that have penetrated into Muslim life over the centuries.

The importance of teaching and training Muslim children to act in accordance with Islamic manners at all times and in all places cannot be over-stated. It is hoped that this book will, *inshā'Allāh*, help to fill the gap noted above, and serve as an accessible handbook to determine what manners suit a particular occasion or circumstance. For ease of reference, each chapter is organized in point form and intended to be complete in itself. Inevitably, where themes common to different chapters are treated, some points have had to be repeated: the alternative, much tedious cross-referencing, we judged to be a greater hindrance to the objectives of the book.

Finally, the author would be grateful to readers for any advice on errors of omission or commission. Comments should be directed to:

Dr. Marwan I. Al-Kaysi,
Humanities Department,
Yarmouk University,
Irbid, Jordan.

1

Introduction

Adab is an Arabic term meaning custom; it denotes a habit, an etiquette, a manner of conduct derived from people considered as models.[1]

During the first two centuries following the emergence of Islam, the term *'adab'* carried ethical and social implications. The root *db* means marvellous thing, or preparation, feast. *'Adab* in this sense was the equivalent of the Latin *urbanitas*, civility, courtesy, refinement of the cities in contrast to bedouin uncouthness.'[2] So *adab* of something means good manner of that thing. The plural is *ādāb*. *Ādāb al-Islām*, therefore, means the good manners adopted by Islam, derived from its teachings and instructions. It is in this sense that it will be used in this book.

Sources

Manners in many cultures other than the Islamic are determined by local conditions and are therefore subject to changes in those conditions. According to W. G. Sumner, 'From recurrent needs arise habits for the individual and customs for the group, but these results are consequences which were never conscious, and never foreseen or intended.'[3]

---

1. F. Gabrieli, *Encyclopaedia of Islam*, new edition. London: Luzac & Co., 1960, Vol. 1, p. 175.
2. *Ibid*.
3. W. G. Sumner, *Folkways*. New York: Blaisdell Publishing Co., 6th printing, 1965, p. 41.

Islamic manners and customs are not in this sense 'unconscious'. They are derived from the two main sources of Islam, namely the Qur'ān and the *Sunnah*, the Prophet's deeds, words and indirect commandments, and are therefore, in the strictest sense, divinely inspired.

The Qur'ān and the *Sunnah* contain the broad principles needed to negotiate the problems that arise in human societies in different ages. As a complete way of life, Islam orders economic, political and devotional activity as well as manners relating to everyday human exchanges and routines. Islam is not confined merely to devotional and legal manners; it embraces criteria and values, attitudes, customs and manners in all reaches of human concern and relationship. As a portion of this whole, Islamic manners are derived from the broad objectives of Islam and reflect its broad ideas and values.

Ādāb al-Islām should neither be conceived nor practised in isolation from the whole. Rather, their interrelation with other elements of Islam should always be kept in mind. Nor, likewise, should the different elements within *ādāb al-Islām* be treated as isolatable, for these too are closely interrelated. To give a single, conspicuous example: a Muslim is required to sleep early so that he may rise early for the *Fajr* (dawn) Prayer.

The divine inspiration of manners in Islam confers on them a religious character which motivates proper adherence. It does not follow from their religious character that every detail of these manners is obligatory. The prescribed manners of Islam vary, in fact, from the 'forbidden' to the 'recommended' – as we shall see in the principal rules of Islamic manners. The former are upheld and enforced by law, the latter do not expose offenders to any formal trial or punishment except in the disapproval of other members of the Muslim community. A third group of manners are those which do not even lead to disapproval if one violates them.

Nor does it follow from the divine origin of Islamic manners that the system should be rigid and inflexible. Islam is not the sort of ideal that is impenetrable to human experience or inapplicable to existing world conditions. Rather, the nature of the system is such that it is flexible in many respects while stable in others, the element of flexibility being grounded in human reasoning to which Islam appeals and which may even be reckoned among its general sources.

The two basic sources of Islam, the Qur'ān and the *Sunnah*, include, besides many detailed rules, general principles which ultimately govern all matters related to the various aspects of life, religious, social, economic, political, etc. None of these general principles are subject to historical change. But conditions do change. The means for deriving rules for new problems in new situations are provided for within Islam in *ijtihād*. *Ijtihād* is the disciplined use of independent individual reasoning to draw the necessary conclusions in accordance with the essence and spirit of Islam and in adherence to its immutable general principles. Thus, through the faith and diligence of qualified scholars, the detail of Islamic teachings can respond effectively to the problem of historical change. The teachings of Islam are, in fact, fully cognizant of human nature and human needs. Islam acknowledges the realities of life and deals with them in the most practical way. There is then no impulse to abrogate or adjust the general principles of the faith in order to adapt them to particular conditions. The realism and practicability of Islamic manners is easily illustrated. For example, fasting the full lunar month of Ramaḍān is a primary obligation upon all Muslims, yet Islam (understanding the vicissitudes of travelling) exempts the traveller from fasting, requiring that he make up lost days when the hardship is over. Likewise, women who have recently given birth, or are in the monthly cycle, and those seriously ill, are similarly exempted. The five daily prayers are, again, a primary obligation, yet the traveller is permitted, according to some *aḥādīth*, to combine certain of the five occasions of *ṣalāt* and perform them together, also to shorten the four-*rakʿah* prayers to two-*rakʿah* prayers, known as *qaṣr*. Islam allows that the precise, final detail of the application of manners may differ, according to the fashions and circumstances of local groups, provided, of course, that the main principles of dress, of dietary laws, etc. are adhered to. Islamic manners are meant to order daily life, to give it rhythm, dignity and serenity; they are not a set of snobbish or legalistic rituals to complicate daily life.

Characteristics: Comprehensiveness and Morality

Islam determines every aspect of the life of a Muslim. This essential fact is very difficult for non-Muslims to grasp. For the believer, Islam gives the criteria for judging all of his behaviour and conduct; it determines his relationship with other individuals, with society as a whole, with the physical world, and it determines also his relationship to his own self. Many examples can be given of what in secular communities are the preserve of arbitrary individual will or the equally arbitrary demands of the social milieu. Food, for example, may be prepared only from what is allowed by Islam; a Muslim can make no use of, for example, pork. A Muslim woman may not uncover her feet in public because in Islam it is not permitted. Goods forbidden to a Muslim, such as wine, may not be exchanged as gifts. If a Muslim is invited to a wedding feast, he should (if physically possible) accept the invitation because it is obligatory to do so. Death-bed wishes may not be fulfilled if they contradict the teachings of Islam, such as a request to allocate an extra share of inheritance to one of the dead person's heirs, or to have his body cremated.

Ādāb al-Islām are a comprehensive code covering almost every aspect of social behaviour, a part of the complete way of life which is Islam. As the different parts of Islam make up an integral unity, the application of ādāb al-Islām in detachment from the rest will not bring about total realization of Islam, indeed it may, in certain respects, become meaningless. The customs and manners discussed in this book are considered suitable for Muslims: those who have a proper religious attitude will instinctively seek to observe the good manners commended or required by Islam.

The various aspects of Islam, ideological, spiritual, legal, social, economic, political, etc., are mutually consistent and supplement each other. For example, faith is essential as it instils in Muslims the spirit of observing the ethical, moral, legal and other prescriptions without external compulsion. Equally, voluntary observance of those prescriptions supports and enhances faith, opening up the path from devotion to social action, linking the two in a strong, stable bond. More specifically the unitary strength of Islam may be seen in, for instance, the manners concerning women, which follow from and sustain the Islamic concept of Muslim womanhood in an Islamic community.

The breadth of *ādāb al-Islām* contrasts sharply with the limitations of 'etiquette'.[4] The manners of Islam are not merely rules of courtesy for various occasions, but cover the whole range of human relations from the simplest actions to the most elaborate of social occasions. The true purpose of Western 'etiquette' (even after it had been extended beyond royal circles to ordinary people) 'seems to have been the protection of the upper class'.[5] By contrast, the true purpose of *ādāb al-Islām* lies in their religious character and nature. They derive from and sustain man's need to remember God in his daily routine; they are designed to keep up his remembrance of God and to help him act rightly and correctly. This is conspicuous in the invocations of God that accompany most everyday incidents of behaviour in Islam. A Muslim should start and end his day, when waking up and when going to sleep, by mentioning God. He should thank and praise God when taking food and drink, when buying

---

4. The origin of 'etiquette' can be traced to the French word 'une etiquette (a ticket), a list of elaborate rules prescribing acceptable behaviour for every situation that might be encountered at court'. *Academic American Encyclopedia*, Danbury: Grolier Inc., 1982, Vol. 7, p. 258.

5. Esther B. Aresty, *Encyclopedia Americana*, Danbury: American Corporation, 1979, Vol. 10, p. 635.

new clothes or other articles of use. Mentioning God is recommended even when relieving oneself. It is recommended to say, when entering the lavatory: 'In the name of Allah. Allah, in You I take refuge from demons', and on leaving the lavatory, ask for His forgiveness. Remembering God and asking Him for perfection and guidance are of special importance when travelling. It may be noted here that the major festivals in Islam are in fact collective celebrations of the successful completion of two principal religious obligations, namely, fasting in the month of Ramaḍān and *ḥajj* (pilgrimage to Makkah).

One of the chief foundations of *ādāb al-Islām* is morality, the cornerstone of a nation's self-confidence and strength, as surely as corruption and immorality are one of the main causes of a nation's decline and disintegration. The insistence on morality often gives to the Islamic way of life an appearance of rigidity or puritanism; as one writer has noted: '. . . in regard to certain aspects of morality, Islam is more rigid and more puritan than certain other systems of life in our times.'[6] But given the importance of morality to the health of a nation, normative Islam is surely right to block all ways leading to corruption, such as illicit sex and luxurious living. Material comforts should not be at the expense of human virtues, individual and collective; politics also (considered, in non-Islamic thought, as immoral or even amoral) must conform to the goals of Islam, the development of human character, the humanity of man.

The ideal of the humanity of man is grounded in the concept of *al-'amāl al-Ṣāliḥ* or virtuous deeds. The term extends beyond what is normally understood as the 'religious' domain and covers a wide range of human activities (in relation to others, to the animate and inanimate environment) sanctioned within Islamic faith and law. The Prophet's life provides many concrete instances: to act justly between

---

6. Muhammad Hamidullah, *Introduction to Islam*. Damascus: The Holy Qur'ān Publishing House, 1977, p. 155.

two people, to help a man onto his mount, to help load his belongings, to speak good words, to remove nuisances from paths or roads, to give food and water to stray dogs and cats, to be forward in greeting others, to visit relatives, etc.; even the act of making love within marriage is valued as a good deed. The most inclusive characteristics of the ideal Muslim personality are humility, modesty and simplicity or naturalness (lack of affectation). Pride and arrogance in any aspect of conduct are not accepted, as no individual is superior to another except in his degree of faith and contribution of good deeds.

Thus, clothes that show haughtiness, that flaunt social status, are forbidden. Manners in eating should demonstrate humility before the occasion as well as respect for the meal: leaning on a cushion while eating is forbidden. Sitting on the floor when eating is a sign of humility, and therefore recommended. Furnishings should show modesty and restraint; for example, the bed should not be set too high above the ground. Gait in walking, manner of address in greeting and in speech generally, should avoid any taint of arrogance.

Islam requires and demands moderation and naturalness in all aspects of life, worldly and religious. Extremism, exaggeration, eccentricity and affectation, caprice and complicatedness are rejected. The insistence on a certain informality in *ādāb al-Islām* is intended to ease their use by the vast majority of the members of the Muslim society. Naturalness of manners is valued as a means of relieving social tension, of enabling and strengthening social relations.

Western 'etiquette' originated in the Royal courts of Europe, and was invented to meet 'the requirement of behaviour in courts and among aristocrats everywhere'.[7] The meaning of etiquette was weakened when it spread to all classes. To this day Western etiquette varies from group to group. Members of so-called 'high society' observe more

---

7. Amy Vanderbilt, *The World Book Encyclopaedia*. Chicago: Field Enterprises Educational Corporation, 1972, Vol. 6, p. 297.

complicated and rigid forms of etiquette than the less well-to-do. This comes out of and helps sustain the class system.

Ādāb al-Islām, however, are different. They are not designed to divide society according to social classes. The rules, revealed through the Qur'ān and the *Sunnah*, were not formulated by certain groups, i.e. the rich and powerful in order to subdue or distance other groups. Islam attaches great importance to the adherence of the whole of Muslim society to its *ādāb*. It does not consider these manners as the privilege or preserve of a certain group, but as a privilege open to every member of the Muslim society. A variety of etiquette levels is non-existent in Islam.

The function of *ādāb al-Islām* in unifying Muslim communities, as well as being an expression of their unity, is clear. But *ādāb al-Islām* are not just about coherence or consistency of behaviour; they are about coherence or consistency of right behaviour. The notion of 'proper' conduct may not, in Islam, be separated from the notion of 'good' deeds, nor from 'faith' and 'devotion'. Faith and good deeds are both necessary in this world for a prosperous and ideal society in which there is mutual and shared responsibility. And in the Hereafter, faith and good deeds are the necessary conditions for forgiveness and salvation, for admission to Paradise. A large number of verses in the Qur'ān link faith and good deeds as defining characteristics of a true Muslim.

Goals

In Islam, what is 'central' and 'essential' is determined by its broad relation to the goals of Islam, among which is the civilization or advancement of human society, the promotion of happiness and prosperity, material as well as moral. On examination, the prescriptions and prohibitions which form part of Islamic teachings will be seen to be not arbitrary decrees but an ordered system of commandments whose purpose (besides testing man's obedience and loyalty to God) is the advancement of man, according to a safe, proper and perfect course, at the individual, family and societal levels. The details of *ādāb al-Islām* are not meaningless formalities, unwelcome to the individual because they are unrelated to the actual needs of his personal or social life. On the contrary, they directly address the different basic functions that concern all members of society at almost every moment of their lives. They are intended to concentrate attention on the central and essential, to rescue man from the peripheral and distracting. They distinguish means from ends and help individual and community to administer personal and collective resources effectively. It may be helpful to illustrate this general point by listing the basic human needs and functions as they are viewed within the perspective of *ādāb al-Islām*:

1. Clothes are primarily intended to protect the wearer against the climate, and to conceal parts of the body.

2. The purpose of housing is to provide shelter from the climate and to secure necessary privacy and safety.

3. Cleanliness, as well as protecting man from disease, expresses his humanity.

4. Adornment, make-up, etc. are a woman's means to look attractive and pleasant before her husband.

5. Speech is important as a means of communication, serving in the essential functions of exchange and relationship with other people, such as buying, selling, etc.

6. Humour reduces tension and relaxes people at a gathering.

7. Gifts are meant to express goodwill and to foster good relations with others.

8. Inviting others to eat, sharing food with others, makes and strengthens social bonds.

9. Social relations themselves are valued because they prevent or limit isolation of the individual. Social customs are valued because they create stability and harmony in social relations.

10. Graves are primarily for honouring the dead, but also to protect the living from the decaying corpse.

11. Animals, in direct relation to man, are intended to be used only for specific purposes such as provision of food, labour, transport. They are not meant to be used by man for his entertainment as, for instance, when animals are set against each other.

It will be immediately obvious that, without the restraint of *ādāb al-Islām*, all these means become ends, destroying a proper sense of values and priorities. Clothes, houses, parties, gifts, drain the resources of individual and community, as people (having lost sight of the true function of these things) spend money in a fruitless endeavour to prove to others their greater purchasing power; in their world the ability to waste goods is a proof of personal success and of the success of the society to which they belong. The consequences of self-adornment or amusement becoming ends in themselves can be measured in the fortunes devoted to these activities by the vast majority in Western countries and, by increasing numbers in Muslim countries. But the real cost of so defying the realities of human accountability under God's law, is the loss of the soul of each individual who hurries fretfully from one escapism to another, seeking to be always excited or distracted and, whenever he catches himself alone, feeling profoundly empty and wretched.

Ādāb al-Islām are designed to avoid such ungrateful waste of human potential, and encourage man to exercise that potential in full conformity with the true purposes and realities of his life. The rules of conduct for a Muslim life contain sound wisdom, whether viewed in religious, cultural, social, economic, psychological or even medical terms. It follows that, for a healthy, balanced life, individual and community should apply these rules comprehensively and conscientiously. Wherever they are applied, two things must always be borne in mind, namely kindness and consideration. Among the root meanings of 'Islam' (besides surrender or submission) is peace; a 'Muslim' is one who has submitted to the decrees of God, who has sought to make peace with God and His creatures. Moreover, the Prophet defines a 'Muslim' as one who does not harm others by hand or tongue.

Kindness and Gentleness

According to a saying of the Prophet, kindness is required in every instance of Muslim conduct. One of the main ends of *ādāb al-Islām* is to train people to be kind and gentle in every matter and toward every thing. The following examples will illustrate:

1. Speaking should be loud enough to be audible to those addressed, never louder.
2. Bad or objectionable language should be avoided.
3. Laughter should not be characterized by loud or unpleasant sounds.
4. Weeping should be restrained and polite, not hysterically loud or abandoned.
5. Eating and drinking should be done at a gentle, dignified pace.
6. It is proper for a Muslim to restrain his anger, keeping himself within the bounds of courtesy.
7. Parents should give their children beautiful, meaningful names, and avoid names indicating difficulty and sadness.
8. Tenderness should be a most essential element in the love-making process.

9. Smiling at other people when meeting them is recommended.
10. Looking pleasantly at others while conversing with them is required as polite conduct.
11. It is necessary that a Muslim be gentle when criticizing others for something they might have done.

Consideration For Others

Inflicting any kind of harm or offence physically, psychologically or morally must be avoided. In the words of the Prophet, 'There should be neither harming nor reciprocating harm.'[8]

Anything done or said with disregard for others is not considered proper Muslim conduct. In fact, good behaviour in Islam depends to a large extent on showing consideration toward others. The contribution of *ādāb al-Islām* in this regard is enormous. Just a few examples will illustrate:

1. Disgracing or reviling others' beliefs, directly or indirectly, is forbidden.

2. The main principle governing one's behaviour on the road is to avoid harming, impeding or disturbing others, including such acts as spitting or making loud noises.

3. Reviling another or speaking of his mistakes is disapproved, even if a Muslim is reviled by him and even though his faults are spoken of by him.

4. Making jokes, using impolite or sarcastic terms at the expense of others, is prohibited. Character assassination through insinuation, backbiting and undesirable conjecture is also prohibited.

---

8. Al-Nawawī's *Forty Ḥadīth*, translated by Ezzeddin Ibrahim: Damascus: Al-Qur'ān Publishing House, 1979, p. 106.

5. Distasteful expressions should be avoided while eating, as they might disturb or upset others.

6. In a group of three people, two should not talk privately as this might offend the third.

7. Reviling the dead is forbidden as this causes hurt to their living relatives.

8. In socializing with others, their comfort and well-being must be positively considered. For instance, neither a person's clothes nor mouth should smell badly; after eating onions or garlic, it is preferable that socializing is avoided.

9. To squeeze between two men in a mosque or to step on others while proceeding to a place, is forbidden, as this will annoy them.

10. To relieve oneself in still water, in the shade, on the road or in any public place, is forbidden, as this might prevent others from making normal use of such facilities and/or be a health hazard.

11. When shoes are taken off, they should be put in a place where they will not disturb others by their smell.

12. When sneezing, the mouth and nose should be covered; when yawning, the hand should cover the mouth; when speaking, one should not speak loudly, as this might annoy others. Even the sitting posture should be such as will not offend others, as does, for example, turning one's back to them.

Role of Ādāb al-Islām in Social Relationships

Among the main aims of *ādāb al-Islām* is to help in establishing and maintaining healthy social relationships. As will be seen, among the necessary attributes of the ideal Muslim personality, are honesty, respect for others, honouring one's word, restraint of anger, patience, modesty, kindness, etc. These virtues eliminate mistrust and create trust, the necessary foundation upon which alone sound relations can be built and developed.

In the Islamic view it is not enough simply to avoid doing harm to others, nor even to wish for others what you wish for yourself. What is required of Muslims toward each other is mutual responsibility and positive assistance.

As will be seen, formality in the manners of Islam is reduced to the barest possible minimum. This enables freer social intercôurse, makes the social machinery run more smoothly and facilitates meetings and visits, for isolation is not recommended in Islam. Muslims are encouraged to meet each other, for that strengthens social bonds and defends the individual against the psychological consequences of social isolation. Moreover, Muslims are encouraged to meet frequently. It is the duty of the host to be hospitable and generous to his guest. Acceptance of an invitation to a meal is recommended and, in the case of an invitation to a wedding meal, acceptance becomes obligatory.

Visiting the sick, taking part in funeral processions, offering condolences to the bereaved, comforting and encouraging them, providing food for them, exchanging gifts with other members of the society, shaking hands when meeting or parting, sharing other happy occasions such as weddings and births, etc., are all ways to strengthen and develop social relations. Particular importance is attached to such exchanges between relatives and neighbours.

Islam has recommended Muslims to hold feasts from time to time and invite others to these occasions. It has also prescribed holding feasts on certain occasions such as weddings, births, the day of Sacrifice, etc. Eating together makes social ties stronger between members of a community irrespective of social status: this is why Islam disapproves of the feast to which the rich are invited and from which the poor are excluded and considers it the worst of feasts.

Social relations should be quite free of personal interest, and engaged in wholly for the sake of God. Thus, a Muslim should not accept a gift presented by someone who intends thereby to influence him favourably. Invitations given out of some personal interest, e.g. in the hope of personal popularity or in expectation of some return, should be rejected.

Social life is encouraged at a wider level, namely by meetings of the community as a whole. It is recommended that the five prayers prescribed in Islam be performed in congregation in the mosque. This provides the opportunity for a large number and variety of people to meet more than once each day. There is the weekly gathering on Friday to perform Friday prayer which, with certain exceptions, is obligatory upon every Muslim. Also, there are the two annual occasions to meet on the feast of *Fiṭr* (breaking the fast) and the feast of *Aḍḥā* (Sacrifice). Moreover, hundreds of thousands of Muslims from all over the world meet every year, for a few days during the pilgrimage season, in Makkah.

The mosque is an important centre where Muslims may discuss religious, social and political issues related to the community and the nation as a whole. Therefore personal matters (e.g. the announcement of lost articles, or other private business) should not be discussed in the mosque. As it is a place for public meeting it should be kept clean – that is the responsibility of every Muslim. Cleanliness and orderliness of the mosque contribute vitally to the success of social meetings held within it.

Personal cleanliness is an important factor when communicating with others, and Muslims are required to bath frequently and, where possible, use perfume, the more so when public occasions (the Friday congregation, for example, or the two *'Īd* festivals, etc.) arise. Especially stressed are those areas of commonest contact, namely the face and hands, and above all the mouth, which deserves to be kept clean and pleasant-smelling because talking is so vital a factor in communication and contact with others.

Religious Aspect of *Ādāb al-Islām*

Islam is based upon *tawḥīd*, the absolute Oneness and Uniqueness of God, and rejects all kinds of polytheism whether primitive or evolved. The *Sharī'ah* is, in fact, the embodiment of this concept, and its every detail springs from it. *Ādāb al-Islām* are consistent with *tawḥīd*, affirming and serving this most fundamental principle. Here are a few examples:

1. Names that mean being a slave of someone other than God, such as *'Abd al-Nabī* (the slave of the Prophet), are forbidden.

2. Reviling natural phenomena, such as wind or rain, which are under God's command, is forbidden. So too is reviling one's fate, or the attribution of injustice to God.

3. Expressions or exclamations that contradict *tawḥīd*, that seem to ascribe partners to God, for example, 'What God wills and what so-and-so wills!' or 'I have no help except from God and you!', are strictly forbidden.

4. Slaughtering animals must be done only for the sake of God; if His name is not taken deliberately, or if some other name is taken instead, the meat of the animal becomes *ḥarām*, forbidden, the sacrifice void.

5. On the occasion of someone's death, expressions that contradict Islamic faith, such as, 'What will become of me now that our source of independence is gone' or 'He died a premature death', are forbidden.

6. Swearing by people or things other than God, His Names or Attributes, is forbidden.

7. A vow pledged for anything or anyone other than God, is null and void and should not be fulfilled.

8. A Muslim is required not to make absolute assertions without referring to God's will, and to say instead *Inshā'Allāh* (If God wills).

9. To bow in respect to any person in not permitted, as bowing is reserved only for God in the act of prayer.

10. To refrain from travelling because some sort of supposed omen against it has been sighted, is forbidden, because this contradicts the principle of belief in destiny.

11. The purpose of visiting the cemetery, which is recommended in Islam, is to remind the living of death, thus influencing them to better their obedience to God and improve their conduct and behaviour in relation to others.

12. The Ka'bah is the first house of God on earth. It was built by the Prophet Ibrāhīm and his son Ismā'īl at Makkah in Arabia. Every Muslim faces the *qiblah* in prayer the world over: it is a symbol of Muslim unity and of the unity of Islam. But it orients more than the Muslim's prayer. When animals are slaughtered they are made to face in the direction of the *qiblah*; deceased Muslims are placed in the grave with their face towards the *qiblah*. Even the design of the lavatory is connected with the *qiblah* in that when relieving himself, a Muslim should avoid facing or turning his back to the *qiblah*.

The contribution of Islamic manners to the unity and solidarity of Muslims will be discussed in greater detail in subsequent pages.

Adherence to the manners of normative Islam will result in the eradication of many *bid'ah* that have penetrated into Muslim life. *Bid'ah* can be defined as an innovated belief or practice added to the original and authentic Islamic belief or practice.

It has been rejected by the Prophet saying, 'He who innovates something in this matter of ours that is not of it will have it rejected.'⁹ And also, '. . . Beware of matters newly introduced (in religion), for every innovation is an error and every error will lead to Hell-fire.'

Anything added and introduced into Islam is considered as *bid'ah* and is therefore rejected. The effect of innovations upon the various aspects of Islamic life is tremendously negative. They transform Islam from being a simple religion to one complicated and difficult to practise, which will lead gradually to the abandonment of at least certain aspects of Muslim life. *Bid'ah* should not be confused with *ijtihād* which is the use of individual reasoning to draw conclusions from the Qur'ān or the *Sunnah* in conformity with the general principles of Islam, and exercised only by qualified scholars.

As mentioned above, many non-Islamic elements have been introduced into the behaviour and manners of Muslims. Here are some examples:

1. Certain religious occasions have been introduced into Islam, such as those of the Prophet's birthday (*Maulid*), his Ascension (*Mi'rāj*), and his Emigration (*Hijrah*).

2. Mentioning God's name audibly and reading the Qur'ān aloud during a funeral procession.

3. Shaking hands following every congregational prayer.

4. The practice that after a certain number of days a bereaved family should prepare food and serve others. The correct Islamic conduct is for friends and relatives to prepare food for the bereaved since they are overwhelmed by sorrow.

5. The practice of plastering and ornamenting graves.

---

9. Al-Nawawī's *Forty Ḥadīth*, p. 40.

Psychological Aspect of Ādāb al-Islām

One of the striking characteristics of *ādāb al-Islām* is that psychological factors are fully taken into consideration. A few examples are:

1. Divorce is highly discouraged during the woman's monthly period, as she is usually passing through a period of psychological tension.

2. Apart from the benefits of hygiene, cleanliness is prescribed in Islam because it refreshes and re-orientates body and mind. This is true in the case of performing ablution before prayer and washing the whole body after sexual intercourse and at the end of childbirth and menstruation. Those who have washed the body of a deceased person are recommended to bathe afterwards. The significance of this advice is that taking a bath in such situations helps to rid people of the psychological effects of those situations.

Medical and Hygienic Aspects of Ādāb al-Islām

Islam teaches Muslims to be always clean and pure. The daily manners of cleanliness and purity of body, place, clothes, etc., contribute enormously to the soundness of bodily health, as reliable medical evidence confirms, for cleanliness prevents the transmission of microbial diseases.

Wuḍū' (the ablution) demanded of Muslims several times every day, as a necessary condition before prayer, requires washing those parts of the body that are generally exposed to dirt and dust.

Paring the nails (ordered by Islam) is to prevent the accumulation of dirt and impurities on fingers which are in constant use for eating and drinking, as well as shaking hands.

Cleaning the axillary and pubic regions from growing hair is also prescribed by Islam. It helps to keep the sweat glands functioning well and prevents the multiplication of the bacteria that would otherwise affect those sweat glands.

Among the impurities from which a Muslim should keep away and purify himself, his clothes, etc. are faeces and urine. The urine contains urea and other nitrogenous compounds which disintegrate into ammonia through the effect of bacteria, giving rise to unpleasant odour. Pinworms (oxyuriasis), viral hepatitis, ascariasis and taeniasisi are among the diseases transmitted mainly through swallowing the infective stage present in faeces.

The fact that the Muslim should not overeat, but should rather stop before his stomach is full, has medical as well as social and moral benefits. The stomach contains stretch receptors; when distended it can give rise to pain and discomfort, as well as more disabling ailments.

When drinking, the Muslim is advised not to breathe into the vessel, for carbon dioxide is present in the expired air in a higher percentage than in the inspired air, and high concentrations of carbon dioxide in the circulation negatively influence several physiological functions.

After drinking milk, the Muslim owes special thanks to God,[10] for the benefit contained in it. Milk is considered adequate nourishment, a complete diet. It contains all the essential nutritional components: carbohydrates, fats, and proteins, in addition to many vitamins and minerals, mainly vitamin D, calcium, phosphate, deficiencies of which cause rickets in children and oesteomalacia in adults.

Slaughtering according to Islamic law provides meat that is clean of blood. Blood is known to be a good breeding ground for micro-organisms which can be the source of many diseases. Besides the health aspect, there is the cultural fact that many people feel disgusted, even ill, when they see meat with blood clotted or oozing amidst the meat fibres. Eating or drinking blood is forbidden in Islam.

Pork is also forbidden in Islam. Pigs are not selective about what they eat and can be fed on garbage, on food remnants. On this subject, Sakr has observed: 'There are a good number of germs, parasites and bacteria that infest swine

---
10. *Mishkāt*, Vol. 2, p. 465.

and live in its flesh which, when it is eaten, transmit diseases to man. Among these parasites are tapeworms, round worms, hook worms, faciolopsis buski, paragonimus, clonorchis senesis and erysipelothrix rhnsiphathiae.'[11] He goes on: 'In short, the pig, the supreme germ carrier, is the cause of many serious and fatal diseases, among them dysentery trichinosis, tape worm, round worm, hook worm, jaundice, pneumonia, suffocation, intestinal obstruction, acute pancreatitis, enlargement of the liver, diarrhea, emaciation, high fever, hindering the growth development in children, typhoid, lameness, heart trouble, abortion, sterility and sudden death.'[12]

Drinking alcohol is prohibited by Islam. Although it has some beneficial effects, it leads to addiction with all its moral and physiological problems. Further, ingestion of large amounts causes irritation of the stomach and peptic ulcer formation. It also affects the liver and causes its inflammation, cirrhosis and ultimately liver failure.

The Muslim is required not to restrain a sneeze, rather to thank God for this blessing. Sneezing results from irritation of the mucous membrane of the upper respiratory tract and it leads to the expulsion of the irritating substance. Prevention of sneezing will retain the irritant which may then cause inflammation where it lodges. Covering the mouth when sneezing is recommended in order to prevent the transmission to other persons of bacteria which may be present in the upper respiratory tract of some individuals.

Circumcision, required of every male Muslim, has been increasingly carried out in some parts of the Western world on medical grounds. The prepuce (a quite redundant piece of skin), if not cut off, can accumulate dirt and organisms which encourage the growth of bacteria. This may be one of the factors causing cancerous changes in the female genital tract.

---

11. A. H. Sakr, *Pork: Possible Reasons for its Prohibition*, published by the author, 1975, p. 15.
12. *Ibid.*, p. 18 (for further microbial and chemical evidence see *Ibid.*, pp. 12–18).

Sexual intercourse during menses, which is completely forbidden in Islam, is harmful for two reasons:

1. The cervix is opened during menses, and intercourse will facilitate the entry of bacteria into the uterus and the fallopian tubes leading to inflammation and formation of adhesions which can cause sterility.
2. The negative psychological effect on the man when he discovers blood on his sexual organ. This may create a sensation of disgust such as to inhibit proper sexual relations with his wife.

The wisdom behind the prohibition of anal intercourse is that it is a painful process and it stimulates the defecation reflex. In addition, the male sexual organ may be soiled with some faeces which may contain pathogenic micro-organisms, in turn causing urinary tract infection in the male.

During the menstrual period the female sexual hormones are disturbed, leading to psychological upset, mainly in the form of nervous tension and depression, and this may explain the changes observed in the behaviour of women during the menstrual period. It partly explains the wisdom of the exemption of women from prayer and fasting.

The fact that, according to Islamic injunctions, the corpse must be buried without delay, shows proper understanding of the dangers of putrefaction: dangers much greater in hot climates where no cooling facilities are available.

The wisdom behind forbidding Muslims to own dogs, except watch and hunt dogs whose place must be outside the house, is clearly seen in the fact that the saliva of dogs contain rabies virus which can be transmitted to man by biting or by contact with the dog's saliva through any cut in the skin. Echinococcus worm is found in the intestine of dogs; transmitted to man through food contaminated with dogs' excreta, it can lead to the formation of cysts primarily in the liver and lungs.

Contribution of *Ādāb al-Islām* to the National Economy

The observance of *ādāb al-Islām* is also essential to a healthy economy; extravagance is forbidden, thriftiness encouraged, even required. Money plays an important role in the life of a nation, both in times of peace and of war. As a store of value it serves as a reserve of ready purchasing power and medium of exchange.[13] Money power is essential for the nation as a whole. The private individual is not absolutely free to spend any amount of money in any way he likes, as this leads to the destruction of this national power. *Ādāb al-Islām* give Muslims a religious motive for saving. In other words, it is the religious duty of every Muslim to abstain from extravagance, for Allah says in the Qur'ān: 'Lo! the squanderers were ever brothers of the devil, and the devil was ever an ingrate to his Lord.'[14]

Here are different aspects of Islamic life which demonstrate the importance that Islam attaches to a healthy economy:

1. Moderation in eating and drinking is required. No food, however little, should be wasted. Forbidding wastefulness saves a large amount of the national wealth, and directs it to more useful investments.

2. Moderation in dress is required. Clothes should not become an end in themselves, and spending large sums of money on clothes should be avoided.

3. Furniture and other household items should be of moderate price. Silver or gold should not be used in domestic furniture or for utensils, or in any other items. Also silk or silk brocade should not be used in furniture or in men's clothes.

---

13. *Encyclopaedia Britannica* (London: William Benton, Vol. 15, 1971), p. 701.
14. *The Holy Qur'ān*, translated by M. M. Pickthall (New York: Muslim World League, n.d.), Sūrah V, verse 3.

4. Large sums of money should not be spent on building lavish houses. Even extravagance in mosque buildings is forbidden. Ornamentation in both cases should also be avoided.

5. In Islam, the ideal wedding is that which involves the least expense and avoids the unnecessary.

6. Funerals should also be inexpensive. Extravagance is forbidden. Coffins should not be used, unless to comply with special regulations or for health reasons.

7. Though generosity and hospitality toward guests is highly recommended in Islam, extravagance is forbidden.

8. Suspending work on Friday is not specifically prescribed in Islam except for about an hour to say the Friday prayers. Useful work should be continued, for to stop working for even a day may cause a loss to the national economy as a whole. Abandoning work on Friday is not encouraged, for the concept of the Sabbath does not exist in Islam. However, if Muslims have to have a day off, it should be Friday and not Saturday or Sunday.

9. Skill and thoroughness in every task entrusted to a Muslim is considered as his duty in Islam: according to the *ḥadīth*, 'Verily Allah has prescribed proficiency in all things.'[15] A successful economy is obvious when industry and quality combine.

Marriage, the Family and *Ādāb al-Islām*

The family 'provides the environment within which human values and morals develop and grow in the new generation; these values and morals cannot exist apart from the family unit. The family system and the relationship between the

---

15. Al-Nawawī's *Forty Ḥadīth*, p. 64.

sexes determines the whole character of a society and whether it is backward or civilised.'[16]

Because marriage and family are so important, it is not surprising that so large a number of Qur'ānic verses and Prophetic Traditions are devoted to these two areas; these sources provide the basis and the details necessary for successful marriage and a morally sound, stable society.

1. A Muslim is recommended to marry at an early age. Marriage enlarges the circle of relatives by adding new ones through the marriage tie. Breast-feeding by foster nurses is permitted in Islam for it too enlarges the circle of the family with new-found relatives, called 'relatives in breast-feeding'.

2. Muslims are encouraged to make marriage an easy task. According to the Islamic view, the most blessed marriage is that which involves the least burden upon the bride and bridegroom.

3. Celebrating marriage has been made commendatory in Islam, for marriage is a social event.

4. Although singing is generally forbidden in Islam, it is allowed on the occasion of marriage.

5. Holding a wedding feast is recommended and rejection of the invitation, when it is possible to accept, is not allowed on this very special occasion.

Islam is concerned that marriages should succeed. They cannot do so unless properly founded. The conditions and recommendations for success are:

1. Full mutual agreement by the man and the woman to marry one another.

2. Common ground and understanding between the man and the woman are obviously necessary. A common

---

16. Sayyid Qutb, *Milestones*. I.I.F.S.O., 1977, pp. 183–4.

conception of life, way of living and common ways of overcoming disagreements is needed, and all these are provided by the Islamic faith and *Sharī'ah*. Therefore, the ideal husband and wife are those who adhere most to Islam.

3. As preparatory steps towards marriage, Islam recommends that the man and the woman should have sufficient information about each other's knowledge and practice of Islam and that they should also see each other.

4. There is no room for any intent on either side to have a temporary marriage. Islam recognizes only the intention to have a lasting marriage.

5. To fulfil all the conditions in any marriage contract is considered by Islam as among the best of deeds and the highest of moral virtues. According to the Prophet: 'The most worthy conditions to be fulfilled by Muslims are those included in a marriage contract.'[17]

6. Husband and wife are advised, in case of disagreements, to try to solve their problems without the interference of anyone else.

7. The husband-wife relationship if it is to succeed must be based upon mutual respect, understanding, co-operation, love and mercy.

A study of *ādāb al-Islām* shows the importance of marriage in Islam. The special relationship of husband and wife is recognized in *ādāb al-Islām* in the following ways:

1. Men are not allowed to wash the bodies of dead women, nor vice versa unless they are married to one another. In the case of a deceased wife the husband has the right to place her body in the grave.

---

17. *Mishkāt*, Vol. 2, p. 171.

2. Men and women are not allowed to see each other's private parts – even though they are related to each other by blood as brother and sister, or mother and children – except in the case of husband and wife.

3. Women are forbidden to mourn a deceased relative including even a brother or father for a period exceeding three days; but a widow may mourn for her dead husband for a period of four months and ten days.

The parent-child relationship also has an important place in the manners of Islam. According to the Prophet of Islam, Paradise lies at the feet of mothers. If good manners toward others are a form of politeness, they are an obligatory religious duty in the case of parents. The conduct of children toward parents, discussed in Chapter 7, shows how heavy is the responsibility imposed upon children in this respect.

Strong kinship, affection, responsibility should not be confined to children and parents, but extended to all relatives. There is, first, the moral responsibility to visit relatives from time to time, to ensure that they do not feel neglected and ignored. Second, there is the financial responsibility upon those more able to assist their needy relatives. If a Muslim dies in debt, his relatives are recommended to discharge the debt as soon as they can.

Allowing breast-feeding by a woman other than the mother, as mentioned earlier, enlarges the circle of relatives, and must be recognized and welcomed in mutual responsibility.

Family feeling and responsibility are so stressed in *ādāb al-Islām* because the family is the formative ground of the whole range of human sentiments, and therefore the best foundation for a healthy, stable society is a healthy, stable family life.

Norms of Sexual Behaviour in Islam

Islam recognizes sex as a portion of nature created by God, and nothing created by Him is evil or wrong if used and practised according to His commands.

There is no doubt that sex is necessary for the development of the individual's personality, and for the society as a whole. Sexual development is intimately connected with feelings of personal worth and the assurance of being loved. Sexual deprivation endangers mental health, hinders good relationships and creates inefficiency in the society. But sex can be a destructive force if not controlled and channelled through marriage. It will then be a force working against the individual, the institution of marriage and family, and the society as a whole. In fact, 'sex is capable of impelling individuals, reckless of the consequences while under its spell, towards behaviour which may imperil or disrupt the co-operative relationships upon which social life depends'.[18]

Sexual behaviour, therefore, must be controlled. This, however, seems difficult, and may indeed be impossible in any society without the assistance of other elements and factors that help the individual to keep sexual desires in check. Islam provides a solution to this problem through the observance of the following rules of conduct:

1. Marriage should be made easy for every member of the society and opportunities for early marriage enhanced.

2. All factors and conditions that incite the individual to indulge his sexual desires outside marriage should be blocked. *Ādāb al-Islām* are vital here:

   (a) The body of the woman is of such a nature that it causes sexual excitement among men. Because this is so and not the other way about, Islam has forbidden all forms of nudity and exploitation of the female form. It prescribes a form of dress designed to cover the whole body except face and

---
18. G. P. Murdock, *Social Structure* (New York: Macmillan & Co., 1949), p. 260.

hands so as to protect the woman from the gaze of men and to protect men from exposure to her charms. There is no doubt that clothes convey inter-personal attitudes among which is that of sexuality.

(b) The separation of the sexes is necessary in Islam. This helps to ease sexual tension.

(c) A Muslim woman should not adorn her face with cosmetics nor use perfume outside the home. Such actions should be confined to her home and for her husband.

(d) Women are not allowed to bathe in a public bath used by men.

(e) When a woman speaks to a man other than her husband or relatives whom she is forbidden to marry (*mahram*), her speech should not be inviting, but should remain objective and crisp.

(f) Showing decorous shyness is also required of men, both in dress and personal conduct. If, by chance, a Muslim's gaze falls upon a woman, he should turn away his eyes: a second look is forbidden.

(g) Privacy in sexual relations is of the utmost importance in the Islamic view. Husband and wife are a mercy to each other, a garment and veil. It is forbidden for either husband or wife to discuss their sexual relations with others.

All the rules given above and others concerning sexual conduct are intended to enable men and women to benefit from the blessings of sex within marriage, and to enable the society to benefit from the blessings of marriage and secure family relations.

Ādāb al-Islām and the Status of Women

When Europe was plunged into its Dark Ages and debated on the nature of woman's soul, on whether or not it was human, Islam had already declared men and women to be of the same origin and nature, equal before God and society, and promised like rewards or punishments for their good or evil deeds.

Islamic law is just and fair for both women and men. A woman in Islam has the right to hold property, and to manage her estates. She has the right to lease, or bequeath, or exploit property for her own benefit.[19] Although a woman's main domain is the house, she is not excluded from making financial transactions such as selling and buying, lending and borrowing, investments, etc. In the different schools of law, women are judged legally competent and fully entitled to carry out any of these transactions.

There is no difference between men and women concerning the penalties accorded under Islamic law whether for drinking alcohol, committing adultery, apostasy or murder.

Women in Islam enjoy the right to express their views freely, and to reject marriage proposals. The contemporary position of Muslim women in some parts of the Islamic world should not be adduced as evidence or argument against the concept and position of women in Islam. The following *ādāb* should remove any misunderstanding on this point:

1. The news of the birth of a girl should be welcomed exactly as the news of the birth of a boy is usually welcomed. It is against the teaching of Islam to convey congratulations on the birth of a boy, but to refrain from doing so on the birth of a girl. Islam stresses the importance of taking special care of daughters.

2. The Prophet exhorts men to treat women respectfully and gently, not to look down upon them as inferior, but to regard them as equals.

---

19. M. Qutb, *Islam the Misunderstood Religion* (Damascus: The Holy Qur'ān Publishing House, 1977), p. 97.

3. Women should be consulted in matters concerning them. The fact that in Islamic marriage there must be a guardian does not mean that he has the right to make the marriage decision. The woman alone has that right, to accept or refuse marriage, free from any pressure. If a girl is betrothed to someone without her consent, she then has the right to approve or disapprove the betrothal.

4. The woman in the role of mother is deeply honoured: we have noted above the Prophet's saying, 'Paradise lies at the feet of mothers.' The one most deserving of loving care by a Muslim is his mother, who commands greater respect than even his father.

5. A married woman may retain her own family name and not necessarily relinquish it in favour of her husband's. This is a mark of respect.

6. Certain manners have been prescribed by Islam in order to protect sexual identity: viz. imitation by men of women in dress, gait, etc. or vice versa, is forbidden.

7. Safeguarding a woman's personality is required in Islam as long as her deeds are not contrary to Islamic teachings. A husband is not allowed to destroy his wife's personality and make it conform to his own.

8. A woman, during her monthly period, may be treated more gently and kindly. A menstruating woman is not considered dirty or sinful as is the case in some other religions and cultures.

9. It is the right of a woman to have sexual intercourse with her husband from time to time. If the husband had never been able to make love to her, then it is her right to have a divorce.

10. A good wife is considered by Islam to be the best asset in the world. She has an extremely important role in

married life – she has responsibility for running the household and the regulation of its economy.

11. Islam requires that Muslim women maintain their cultural identity and do not imitate the manners of non-Muslim women in dress, shoes, etc. Such imitation is a clear indication of weakness.

12. In Islam, a woman's dress has to serve certain purposes among which is the protection of her honour and integrity. The difference between men's and women's dress is due to the difference between the male and female forms and the sexual effect of that difference. For the same reason, a woman may not undertake a journey unless accompanied by her husband or a *mahram* (a consanguine relative whom the law forbids her to marry).

Ādāb al-Islām and Discipline

Islamic manners train and educate the individual to control his passions and to respond to the voice of reason. They also educate him to exhibit qualities of patience, of being content and of self-dependence, that is, not seeking the help of others unless unavoidable.

One of the most praised virtues in Islam is the ability to control one's anger and not react violently. In the words of the Prophet, a powerful human being is one who controls himself when he is angry.

Punctuality and self-discipline are also valued as most important characteristics of a good Muslim. The five daily prayers teach punctuality, and the month of fasting teaches sustained self-control.

The fruits of discipline are (a) moderation and (b) wise use of time. Moderation is one of the main aims of *ādāb al-Islām,* for it creates a life of balance and equilibrium, which is necessary if a man is to be of service to others (for how can anyone given to exaggeration or affectation ever be sufficiently free of himself to help others disinterestedly) and if he is to serve God in all that He commands? Time is a human measure of the value of the life God has given: one of the most crucial questions that every man will be asked on the Day of Resurrection is what use he made of his time. Therefore, it is the responsibility of every Muslim to make the best use of every minute, to weigh every grain, for his own interest and for the interest of the nation as a whole.

Ādāb al-Islām are prescribed so as to be in full conformity with the above-mentioned principle. The following clarify this point:

1. Muslim daily life begins at dawn before sunrise, and ends early just after ṣalāt al-'ishā' (the night prayer), that is, about one and a half hours after sunset.

2. Socializing for the sake of passing the time is disapproved. Although it is recommended that Muslims meet one another frequently, they should make use of these meetings to discuss useful matters.

3. Spending an unnecessarily long time eating should be avoided.

4. Moderation in speaking is required. Speaking at length or just for the sake of it is a bad habit and considered a waste of time: silence is preferable.

Concern About Human Safety

It is notable that Islam concerns itself with the safety of individuals. Below are some familiar ādāb, but any conduct that assists in achieving this purpose and does not contradict the principles of Islam is considered as part of ādāb al-Islām. The following are recommended:

1. Before going to bed, one should make sure that doors are properly closed, food pots and drinking vessels covered, and all sources of fire extinguished or turned off.

2. Sleeping on the roof of a house where there is no protecting wall or in a lonely place with nobody else around in case of emergency, should be avoided. Also, mattress and pillow should be examined to ensure that no harmful insects have hidden under or inside them.

3. Before drinking from any vessel, one should check that nothing harmful has fallen into it.

4. Travelling should, as far as possible, be undertaken in company and not alone. No vehicle should be so parked as to obstruct, hinder or endanger others.

5. Before putting on shoes, they should be checked to ensure that no harmful insect has hidden in them during the night or while they have been in disuse.

6. Certain animals, considered pests, are harmful to man, and for that reason should be killed: examples are scorpions, mice and snakes.

Ādāb al-Islām for the Preservation of Unity and the Cultural Identity of Muslims

One of the great achievements of *ādāb al-Islām* has been their contribution to the unity of Muslim peoples who belong to different races, speak different languages, and inhabit different parts of the globe. The religious character of Islamic manners, derived from the Qur'ān and the *Sunnah*, plays an important role in this respect. Thus a Moroccan who travels to Pakistan will not find it difficult to understand the manners of the people there, nor feel out of place. Muslim women from Egypt will not be astonished by the sight of Turkish women wearing Islamic dress. Members of the Islamic society reassert their solidarity on each occasion of each day that they adhere to the ways of doing things which constitute their very tradition. *Ādāb al-Islām* create common understanding among Muslims – they form a universal culture which gives shape and meaning to local cultures throughout the world. The local culture may well differ from one Islamic community to another. By contrast, the system of prayers, greetings, major festivals, dietary restrictions (e.g. on alcohol), the practice of *ḥarām* and *ḥalāl*, are elements of the universal Islamic pattern. Conspicuous too is the fact that everywhere Muslim women dress modestly and in most Muslim countries wear the proper Islamic dress. The local variations (e.g. in national dishes, such as *biryānī*, popular in the Indian subcontinent, or in dress, such as the *sārī* as worn by Muslims in India) are important in that they distinguish one group of Muslims from another – we are created in different nations, the Qur'ān tells us, that we may know one from another – but they are completely insignificant in the sense that they do not diminish the Muslim character and Muslim identity of the particular group.

An important rule of *ādāb al-Islām* is the prohibition against imitating the manners of non-Muslim peoples. This should not be confused with seeking knowledge, in crafts, technology, science, etc. which has always been encouraged by Islam. Manners play a vital part in the maintenance of cultural identity. It is obvious that manners embodying a Muslim life should be distinguished from others by their own Islamic character.

Any intrusions of non-Muslim cultures into Muslim life do not mean that Islamic identity is being erased. This is because the Islamic way of life is so deeply ingrained that a Muslim cannot easily rid himself of it, and it is so deeply ingrained because it is *not* a temporary improvisation of forms in response to a particular period of history but a stable structure of interrelated manners and ideals that conform to the unchanging realities of human relations between man and man, and between man and God. Let whoever doubts this consider the different states of Christianity and Islam in the Soviet Union, hated and suppressed alike by the ideology of Russian communism. No; despite the economic and political disunity that prevails on the surface, the cultural strength and unity of Islam is still a reality throughout the Muslim world.

Islamic Attitude Toward Manners and Customs of Non-Muslims

The tolerance shown by Muslims toward non-Muslims living in Muslim lands is without parallel. Islam affords protection to the religion and culture of every community within the Islamic state. Any conversion to Islam must be through free choice and conviction.

The life, property and honour of every non-Muslim individual is fully protected by Islam. Moreover, Islam has guaranteed full religious autonomy and limited judicial authority to its non-Muslim citizens. Non-Muslims have the following rights:

1. Full freedom of belief and worship, and independent religious and educational institutions.

2. Full autonomy concerning personal and family law including the rules of marriage and divorce though opposed to Islamic rules.

3. In financial, transactional and civil affairs, treatment equal to that of Muslim citizens, except in certain cases, e.g. drinking alcohol, for which they may not be punished, provided it is not done in public.

4. In social customs, non-Muslims are free to preserve their distinct character as expressed, for example, in modes of dress (as long as they do not contradict Islamic law), eating and diet.

The refusal of Islam to impose its own *ādāb* on non-Muslims has helped to avoid communal frictions and religious strife; European rule, by contrast, has exploited and exacerbated community differences for the sake of political or military advantage.

There are some restrictions upon Muslims concerning their social relations with non-Muslims. These restrictions are self-explanatory – the religious occasions of non-Muslims are not part of a Muslim's faith, though it is a part of his Islam to tolerate them; it follows that he should not participate in them. Far from indicating fanaticism or intolerance these restrictions express a balance between tolerance, even respect, and the need to preserve the distinctness and stability of Muslim belief, practice and *ādāb*.

The tolerance of Islam is particularly striking when compared to the intolerances inflicted upon Muslims in non-Muslim lands or under non-Muslim authority. For example, in the sixteenth century, following the collapse of Muslim rule, the Christian courts of the Inquisition burnt to death all Muslims who refused to abandon their faith and convert to Christianity. Muslims were forced to change their names, dress and customs and to behave according to Christian manners.

A further example from history is the case of the Jews who, in various parts of Christian Europe, were forced to change their clothes, names and customs to conform to Christian tradition, but who, in the Muslim world, were treated with a unique tolerance. They were allowed to practise and maintain their religious rituals and customs according to their own traditions. The golden age of Jewish literature took place during Muslim rule in Spain. When the Muslims left Spain, the Jews left with them.

The evidence of this difference in treatment is still to be found today. The Jews who have lived in the Muslim world, whether they are still living there or have migrated to Israel, have Jewish names, while those who lived or are still living in the Western world have Russian, English, German or French names.

Overview of the Principal Rules of Islamic Conduct

The Islamic day has a character perhaps surprisingly different from the day as it looks and is experienced in non-Islamic countries. It begins very early (i.e. after the *Fajr* prayer) and also ends very early (i.e. after the *'Ishā'* prayer). As the Islamic calendar is lunar, dates are determined according to the moon, not the sun, with the months moving round from year to year. Time is precious for the Muslim, and he must apportion each day wisely. Quotidian problems and difficulties are put aside to observe the prayers at the five prescribed times and observing them mitigates the intensity of these problems, setting them into proper perspective. But since that perspective is Islam it applies throughout the day. For, unlike other religions, Islam influences a Muslim's conduct from the moment he rises until the moment he retires for the night. These influences of course vary in degree, the variations broadly classifiable into five categories:

1. What is permitted – most actions fall into this category.
2. What is recommended.
3. What is disapproved or abhorred.
4. What is obligatory.
5. What is forbidden.

It is interesting to note that only a very small percentage of man's actions fall into the categories of obligatory and forbidden. The dividing lines between these five categories are flexible. What is forbidden under one set of conditions may become, under another, an exceptional set of conditions, permissible or even obligatory. For instance, Muslims are forbidden to eat pork. But if a Muslim finds himself faced with starvation and all that is available for him to eat is pork, then, to save his life, he is allowed to eat it.

The general rules that govern Muslim conduct have not simply been arbitrarily dictated; they are derived from the Qur'ān and the *Sunnah* of the Prophet; both are divinely inspired and intended as a mercy to mankind. No Muslim may be taken to task if he commits a breach of Islamic tenets or laws, if there was an unavoidable and compelling reason resulting either from his own condition or from external compulsion.

Although practising Islam is not absolutely obligatory until the individual has passed the age of puberty, it is nevertheless recommended that children grow up in an Islamic atmosphere, thus facilitating their practise later.

The principal characteristics and rules of Islamic manners for various aspects of life can be summarized as follows:

1. In almost everything, deliberation (and not haste) is required. A Muslim should consider how a matter may turn out; then, if the outcome appears worthwhile and good, he should carry on, otherwise he should refrain.

2. Kindness and gentleness in a Muslim's dealings with others are essential.

3. Cleanliness and purity of body, place, clothes, etc., should be one of the most conspicuous characteristics of Muslim life.

4. Beauty, elegance, orderliness are values for the Muslim to observe, and whenever possible to attain.

5. According to Islam, a good deed done with courtesy beautifies that deed; impudence, on the other hand, destroys the good in it.

6. All a Muslim's deeds should express an attitude of humility and not arrogance.

7. A Muslim is commanded to avoid any act that might harm himself or some other person, physically, mentally or morally.

8. In the daily life of a Muslim, silence is preferred to unnecessary speaking.

9. A Muslim should treat others as he would wish them to treat him. Like for others what he would like for himself. Good manners without consideration for others are an impossibility.

10. A Muslim should never order or ask anyone to do something that he would not do himself.

11. Favouring the right side or hand in things such as giving, taking, shaking hands, eating, drinking, walking, etc., and using the left hand for such things as cleaning oneself in the toilet, is recommended.

12. Eating, drinking and clothing oneself, etc., well, are allowed as long as the motive is not pride or arrogance. Life characterized by extravagance is abhorred.

13. Though extravagance is abhorred, this does not imply that a Muslim should not have money or not enjoy life. The effects of God's blessings upon him should be visible to others.

14. Being generous and not mean or avaricious is a virtue.

15. Gratitude to God should characterize a Muslim's life, whether He blesses or burdens him, and gratitude with patience and fortitude.

16. A Muslim must be always faithful.

17. In all aspects of life a Muslim must exercise moderation and be natural; unnaturalness and exaggeration are disapproved.

18. A Muslim should be self-sufficient and should seek the help of other Muslims only when it is urgent and necessary.

19. Copying or imitating other cultures and religions in any way is forbidden.

20. Obedience and carrying out another's orders or wishes may not contradict the teachings of Islam; if it does, the teachings of Islam must be given priority.

21. Maintaining sexual identity is most important. Imitation of men by women, or of women by men, in dress, manner of walking, etc. is forbidden.

22. One of the most pervasive characteristics of Islamic manners is discipline, leading to balance and harmony in the life of the individual and the community.

23. Flexibility and tolerance are also characteristics of *ādāb al-Islām*. Broadly speaking, any particular conduct is tolerated or accepted if it is civilized (i.e. considerate of others) and respectable (i.e. inoffensive to the individual and community) and provided it does not fall into the categories of the abhorred or forbidden.

2

Bodily Functions

Sneezing

Sneezing[1] is considered in Islam a blessing from God. The manners concerning it are these:

1. A Muslim should not seek to restrain or prevent a sneeze; it is a healthy function. In any case, sneezing cannot be done at will, nor can it be easily suppressed.[2]

2. When about to sneeze, a Muslim should turn his face away or cover his mouth and nose with hand or handkerchief, thus lessening the noise and, at the same time, avoiding nuisance to those nearby.

3. Since sneezing is considered a blessing from God, a Muslim should acknowledge this by saying: *Al-ḥamdu lillāh* (Praise and thanks to God).

4. When a Muslim sneezes and praises God, those who hear the praise should invoke a blessing on him by saying: *Yarḥamuka Allāh* (May God have mercy on

---

1. 'It is a reflex spasm of chest and pharynx muscles that causes expulsion of air through the nose. Like the coughing reflex which expels air through the mouth, the sneezing reflex is a protective mechanism for the breathing passage. In the nose, instreaming air is breathed to produce conditions the lungs will tolerate. The air is heated to approach body temperature, humidified to near saturation, and purified of contaminant bacteria and particles, so that air entering the windpipe is usually sterile and particle-free.' *Encyclopedia Americana*, Vol. 25, p. 107.
2. *Ibid.*

you), to which the proper response is: *Yahdīkum Allāh wa yuṣliḥ bālakum* (May Allah guide you and grant you well-being).

5. It is right to invoke a blessing on one who sneezes at the most three times. If he sneezes more often, this probably means he has a cold.

6. If a Muslim sneezes and does not praise God, invoking a blessing on him is not required.

7. If a Muslim sneezes and forgets to praise God, then it is the duty of Muslims near him to remind him kindly of his duty to thank God.

8. Blessings for a non-Muslim who sneezes should be expressed in the words: *Yahdīkum Allāh* (May God guide you on the Right Way).

Yawning

Yawning[3] is considered to be bad and as far as possible should be suppressed. A Muslim should:

1. Try to refrain from yawning as much as possible.

2. When yawning hold his hand over his mouth.

3. Try not to make any sound when yawning.

---

3. 'An involuntary deep inspiration of air into the lungs, often accompanied by stretching of the arms and legs. Precipitating factors include extreme fatigue, boredom, the observation of the act of yawning in others, poor ventilation with reduced oxygen supply, and certain disease processes which produce decreased blood flow to the cerebral cortex. The act of yawning involves all the muscles of respiration beginning with the diaphragm and extending to the abdominal musculature, intercostals and trunk musculature, the scalenus, and infrahyoid muscles in the neck. If the mouth is inadvertently opened too wide in yawning, the jaws may become dislocated or the neck muscles under the chin, particularly the omohyoid, severely strained.' *Encyclopedia Americana*, Vol. 29, pp. 655–6.

Going to Bed

Necessary Preparation

1. A Muslim should be sure to relieve himself before going to bed.
2. It is recommended to go to bed in a state of purity by performing *wuḍū'* (partial ablution).
3. It is preferable, and hygienic, not to go to bed on a full stomach.

When to Sleep

1. Going to bed before *'ishā'* prayers is inadvisable lest the prayer be missed.
2. Sleeping during a period of the day when a prayer time has begun should be avoided, unless the prayer be said first, again for fear that the prayer may be missed.
3. For those who can afford it a brief siesta between the *ẓuhr* and *'aṣr* prayers is recommended. This helps to relax eyes and body and refreshes the person for the day's work that remains.
4. Except to fulfil some necessary duty or to entertain a guest, a Muslim should retire to bed directly after *'ishā'*. In this way he will be refreshed and able to get up with the dawn and make full use of his day.

The Bed

1. The bed should be of simple design and construction. It should be neither too comfortable nor too uncomfortable; comfortable enough to provide the necessary relaxation without encouraging torpor or indolence.
2. The bed should not be set too high off the ground – this in the interest of humility.

3. The bed should not be so placed that part of the body is in the sun and part in the shade.

4. Security is important, therefore any roof area which lacks a protecting wall should be avoided. Likewise, lonely places where help cannot reach in the event of some emergency like sudden illness, attack from intruders, or fire.

5. In the absence of a bathroom close by, as happens in rural areas, it is not forbidden to have a suitable vessel under the bed in which to pass water. This is obviously useful to the sick and elderly and those sleeping out of doors.

When Going to Sleep

A Muslim should observe the following rules:

1. Examine mattress and pillow to ensure that no harmful insects, etc. have hidden inside them.

2. Pray with the words: *Bismika Allāhumma ahyā wa bismika amūt* (In Your name, O God, I live and die).

3. Sleep on his right side and avoid sleeping on his left side.

4. Never sleep on his stomach.

5. Should not try to force himself to sleep. Sleep should occur as naturally as possible, according to the body's needs.

6. Make mention of God, and keep mentioning Him till sleep comes. This will help him relax and prevent thoughts of the day's difficulties and problems.

7. Regulate his sleeping to conform to his body's real needs, neither more nor less.

When Awakening

1. Wake up with the dawn. The positive psychological effect on the whole day of doing so is clear and understood by those who experience it.
2. Start the new day as he ended the previous day by mentioning God, praising and thanking Him.
3. Clean his teeth with a toothbrush or tooth stick (*miswāk*) when he gets up before performing *wuḍū'* for *fajr*, as also if he wakes up in the night for any length of time.
4. If no running water is available, then, when he wakes, pour water over his hands first, before dipping his hand into a retaining vessel for water. This is because he does not know what his hand has touched during the night.

When Having Dreams and Nightmares

1. To pretend to have had a dream which he did not is a sin: Islam rejects all forms of lying.
2. If he sees in a dream what he likes, then he should recount it only to someone whom he likes. If he sees what he dislikes, then he should seek refuge in God from its evil and from the evil of the devil.
3. Talk about dreams only to a friend or to someone of sound judgement.
4. Dreams are for the individual who had them and not for others. If a Muslim feels he has seen the Prophet, upon him be peace, and/or received from him some kind of instruction or advice, he must keep it to himself and must not divulge it to others. Islam is complete and has never acknowledged dreams as a source of Islamic teachings.

Relieving Oneself

The proper place is either one especially designed and built or a 'lavatory' improvised out of doors. The following should be observed:

1. A Muslim should enter the lavatory with his left foot first, saying: *Bismillāh Allāhumma Innī a'ūdhu Bika min al-Khubthi wa al-Khabā'ith* (In the name of Allah. Allah, in You I take refuge from all evils).

2. One should not go to the lavatory in company, nor seek it there; nor should private parts be uncovered to others, as in men's rest rooms where men stand beside each other and urinate into fixtures placed for this purpose. A non-transparent screen between such fixtures is necessary.

3. The lavatory must not be entered with unprotected feet. This is to avoid transfer to the body of impurities and dangerous micro-organisms.

4. One should not begin to undress before entering the lavatory. Maximum privacy and decency is a necessity.

5. Purification afterwards is necessary. This can be done by washing with water after urinating, and by using toilet paper and then washing with water in the case of a bowel movement.

6. It is recommended that, when relieving oneself or washing afterwards, the right hand should not be used. This is in accordance with the Islamic way of devoting and confining the use of the right hand to good things such as eating, drinking, holding the Qur'ān, etc. and confining the left hand to other things such as washing after relieving oneself, blowing one's nose, etc.

7. Though taking care to avoid getting impurities on body or clothes, and washing afterwards, are necessary, exaggeration and obsessive squeamishness in either should be avoided.

8. It is indecent for a Muslim to look at his private parts and his excretion.

9. For a Muslim to urinate or relieve himself in the direction of the *qiblah* is forbidden. Neither is facing nor turning his back to the *qiblah* allowed, therefore turning towards the other two directions is required. This rule applies to all lavatory places indoors or out.

10. Squatting is the best posture when passing water, though standing to do so is not forbidden if squatting causes physical difficulty (as in the case of the elderly).

11. For a Muslim to talk while relieving himself is considered un-Islamic except in the case of real need. Likewise, reading while relieving himself.

12. If someone greets a Muslim while he is relieving himself he should not respond till he leaves the lavatory; then he should apologize to him and return the greeting.

13. A Muslim should leave the lavatory only after covering his body correctly.

14. It is recommended that a Muslim does not pass water in the same place as he bathes.

15. On coming out of the lavatory, a Muslim should say: *Ghufrānaka* (O God, grant me forgiveness).

Outdoors

There are certain rules for a Muslim when relieving himself outdoors, in places such as forests, deserts, camping sites:

1. It is forbidden to do so in still water, in the shade, on the road or where people walk, in any cavity that may serve some animal or reptile as a dwelling, and in a windy place. This is in accordance with the Islamic principle, 'There should be neither harming nor reciprocating harm.'

2. It is necessary for him to conceal himself and go where he will not be seen naked.

3. It is wise to use such ground as avoids any risk of soiling himself or his clothes.

Menstruation[4] and Child-Bed

Menstruation and child-bed should be represented and treated as normal events that need not restrict a woman from leading a normal life. The few restrictions imposed upon women in these two states are as follows:

1. Performing prayer, fasting, reading the Qur'ān and staying at a mosque are forbidden.

2. Circumambulation of the Ka'bah is also forbidden, even for women performing pilgrimage who have become menstruous. These may perform all rituals of the pilgrimage except the circumambulation. The same restriction applies to men in a seminally defiled state.

3. Sexual intercourse is also forbidden. A woman's husband may embrace and kiss her and touch her above the waist if he wishes.

4. When her monthly period comes to an end, a woman may fast, but not pray until after she has taken a bath. After bathing she is required to make up for the fasting days missed during Ramaḍān, but not for prayers missed.

5. It is the duty of every Muslim woman after menstruation or child-bed is ended to take a bath, washing the whole

---

4. 'Menstruation is the periodic discharge of blood and bloody fluid from the uterus. It is a phase of the egg-production cycle in women. It is associated with the degeneration of the lining of the uterus. Many girls begin to menstruate at 11 years of age or earlier, while others do not start until they are 16 or older, but the main age is between 13 and 14. There is a great variation in the number of days of menstruation, but in most cases the flow lasts three to five days.' *Encyclopedia Americana*, Vol. 18, p. 636.

body and hair; it is recommended that she applies musk (or other perfume if musk is unavailable) with a cloth to her private parts. After bathing she can make all observances forbidden during menstruation or childbed.

6. A man should treat his menstruating wife in a normal way.
7. Menstruous women are allowed to attend the Feast prayer though not to participate in it, provided the prayer is not held in the mosque.

Man's Seminally Defiled State

A man who has become seminally defiled either during sleep, or love-making, or by any other means, is required to take a bath as soon as possible. While he is in a defiled state, before taking a bath, he may not pray, recite the Qur'ān, or touch it, circumambulate the Ka'bah or stay at a mosque.

The same rule applies to a woman who has become seminally defiled either during sleep or through sexual intercourse, including the case where her husband penetrates her but does not ejaculate.

3

Cleanliness and Purity

One of the attributes symbolizing man's progress and demonstrating his humanity, as well as distinguishing him from the animals, is cleanliness.

Impurities

It is demanded of a Muslim that he keeps away from impurities and purifies himself, his clothes, his 'place' or immediate environment. These impurities are, for example, emetic, prostatic fluid, urine, intoxicants, human excrement, droppings of animals, blood, pus, and milk of animals forbidden as food. Whatever is severed from living animals is considered impure except parts of fish and locusts, and the wool of sheep, goat and camel. All animals are considered impure if they are not slaughtered according to the Islamic way.

If any such impurities have fallen onto a Muslim's body or clothes or 'place', then washing them off is an obligatory duty.

Bathing

1. Cleanliness of the human body is essential for various reasons. In addition to protecting the body against disease, it is an important factor when communicating with others in the society.

2. Taking a bath from time to time is, therefore, the way to avoid smelling bad.

Where to Bathe

1. Men can bathe in a public bath, provided either they use a curtain or wear a lower garment.
2. Urinating in a bathing place should be avoided if the ground is of earth, as this will accumulate impurities; if it is a tiled floor and has drainage, it is not forbidden.

When Washing is Obligatory

Washing the whole body becomes necessary:

1. After seminal emission – this applies also to emission during sleep or a dream – to remove sexual defilement.
2. For a woman who has a sexual dream provided she sees signs of liquid; for a woman at the end of her menstrual period, and at the end of child-bed.

There are, in addition, special occasions when washing is recommended. These are the two Festivals in Islam, on embracing Islam, and every Friday before the congregational prayer.

Method of Washing

A Muslim should observe the following:

1. Before he starts to wash, he should be sure he has concealed himself from others.
2. Place his clothes and towel in a clean place.
3. As a first step, remove impurities before he begins washing.
4. Wash his hands three times.

5. Rinse his mouth and take water up into his nose.
6. Wash his face and arms.
7. Pour water on his body, beginning with the right side.
8. Be sure that water has reached every part of his body and hair, and let the water run between his fingers and toes.
9. When using soap, this must be followed by clean water so that none of the soap remains on his body. This is required when washing is obligatory.
10. Bathing in a bath tub is permitted, provided that he follows this by taking a shower to guarantee that all impurities have been removed.

Importance of Cleaning Certain Parts of the Body

Cleaning certain areas of the body where dirt mainly accumulates is necessary, such as:

1. Shaving off pubic hairs, whenever necessary.
2. Plucking out hairs under the armpits. If that is difficult then shaving can be substituted.
3. Paring the nails: when paring the nails is necessary, a Muslim should start with his right hand, then his left hand, his right foot, and finally his left foot.

Keeping other parts of the body clean, in particular the face, head, hands and feet is of special importance. Doing so is especially refreshing to body and mind; moreover these are the parts most commonly in contact with other people.

Special attention should also be given to cleaning the mouth, which is used in communicating with others.[1] Two complementary ways of keeping the mouth clean and pleasant smelling are:

---

1. It has been found that the oral cavity contains more micro-organisms than the anal region, and therefore one is advised by dentists to keep the mouth clean, especially after meals, by brushing the teeth, to get rid of any food remnants.

1. Using a toothpick following meals.
2. Using the *miswāk* (tooth stick) or a toothbrush, starting from the right side of the mouth.

Any one of these methods is not a substitute for the others; they complement each other. It is difficult and impractical to carry a toothbrush everywhere; a *miswāk* or a tooth stick, on the other hand, may be taken anywhere easily. In addition, a *miswāk* can be readily used when meeting someone, when the smell of the mouth changes, and when returning home from work.

Cosmetics and Adornment for Men

There are special rules for women, others for men, and still others common to both sexes.

Hair

1. Having a part of the head shaved and leaving a part unshaven is not an Islamic way of hairdressing. It should either be all shaved or all left.
2. Attention to and care of hair – cleanliness and tidiness, i.e. combing it, using hair oil, keeping the comb clean, etc. – is Islamic conduct. However, this should not be exaggerated.
3. There is no special Islamic hair style. However, the Prophet used to have three styles of hair: *wafra* (hair extending beyond the lobe of the ear), *limma* (hair descending below the lobe of the ear) and *jumma* (hair extending to the shoulder joints).

Beard

1. The beard is an element of beauty on a man's face, so it should be left unshaven.
2. A beard should be kept clean and combed.
3. A man should not be ashamed of grey hairs in his beard, and should not pluck them out.

Perfume

1. The best kind of perfume is musk oil. A man should perfume himself from time to time. If somebody offers him a perfume, it is better to accept it and not to reject it, as it is considered a good thing.

Moustache

1. A moustache should not be allowed to grow too long. It should be clipped so that the upper lip is visible.

Signet Ring

1. Having a ring is permissible for a Muslim, even for those who are not married or engaged.
2. It is forbidden for men to wear gold rings. In fact gold must not be used by men except for medical or dental purposes.
3. The ring can be made of any metal except iron and gold. It should preferably be made of silver.
4. The ring may be worn on the fingers of the left or the right hand.

Women's Make-Up and Adornment

1. There is nothing more fitting than for a woman to leave her beauty as it is, natural, without changes or additions.

2. A woman is, however, allowed to beautify herself provided that she does so at home. A woman should make herself beautiful at home for her husband, by beautifying her face with cosmetics, by keeping herself clean and by having a pleasant fragrance.

3. It is permissible for a woman to stain her hands with henna (a red plant-dye).

4. It is permissible for a woman to use perfume in the presence of male relatives whom she is forbidden to marry.

Hair

1. A woman should try to keep her hair clean and tidy. In fact, hair for a woman is just like a beard for a man, i.e. a significant element of beauty.

2. If a woman has short hair, she should not try to add false hair. If another lady asks her to help her fix false hair on her head, she should refuse.

Face and Hands

1. A woman should take special care to keep her face clean.

2. If hairs have grown on a woman's face, she must neither be ashamed of it, nor try to remove them, nor pull out hairs for another woman. She must not be ashamed of her nature.

3. A woman should never tattoo another woman or have herself tattooed.

4. A woman should never pluck her eyebrows.
5. Nails should not be allowed to grow long; they should be pared frequently.
6. Make-up for ladies is forbidden outside the home, with the exception of black antimony on the eyes.
7. Such things as sharpening the ends of the teeth and making spaces between them for the sake of beauty, are not allowed.
8. A woman should keep her mouth clean and healthy.

Perfume

1. A woman is allowed to perfume herself only indoors and provided no stranger or non-*mahram* relative is there.
2. A perfumed woman may not leave her home unless she has got rid of the smell of perfume. Any adornment that may be inviting to strange men is forbidden, as this is a step to corrupting the society.

General Guidelines for Both Sexes

1. Grey hair may be dyed any colour, except black. The preferable colours are blonde, red and henna.
2. Antimony may be applied, from time to time, for it clears the sight, and gives the eyes beauty.

4

Table Manners

The Meal

To prepare a good table, it is necessary to concentrate on cleanliness, tidiness and moderation concerning the amount of food and the variety of dishes.

1. Food should be prepared from only lawful ingredients. Pork, alcohol, anything containing gelatine taken from a pig, sweets made with alcohol, blood, animals forbidden in Islam such as snake and frog, animals slaughtered in a non-Islamic way are *ḥarām*, unlawful to consume.

2. Cooking vessels belonging to non-Muslims should be thoroughly cleaned before use. This is because Muslims have special instructions on cleanliness and food, which others are not expected to follow.

3. Cooking a little extra broth is recommended since it will help to feed more people. Also, filling vegetables, such as squash, may be prepared, since this is an economical way of enlarging a meal and so satisfying the hunger of more people.

4. If onions or garlic are liked they should be used in cooking, but should not be eaten raw as this gives rise to mouth odour which is unpleasant for others.

5. Using silver or gold tableware is forbidden.

6. Milk and honey are the best foods. The best part of an animal is the meat from its back.

7. Food should preferably be taken while sitting on the floor, as this is a sign of humility.

8. Considering the consumption of meat (including beef) to be forbidden is itself forbidden.

9. Setting the table in Islam differs from the method used in other cultures. The Islamic table is characterized by cleanliness, simplicity and moderation; beauty is also a recommended characteristic, provided it does not result in a waste of time and energy, as is often the case in Western etiquette. Meals should be considered a means of nourishment and not an end in themselves.

Sitting Down to Eat

1. A Muslim should be humble to God while sitting to eat, respecting His Grace. Although there is not a particular prescribed form of sitting, there are conditions, of which humility is the most important.

2. A Muslim should not eat while lying on his back or stomach and should avoid eating while standing or walking.

3. When eating, a Muslim should be properly seated and should not lean on a cushion or on his hand.

4. Sitting to eat should be so arranged that excessive amounts of food and of time are avoided.

5. He who misbehaves while eating, such as by eating with his left hand or using foul language or eating from other people's side of the platter, should be reprimanded.

Proper Table Manners

1. There is no objection to taking meals alone, thought it is better if the family gathers together for dining

because, it is believed, food tastes better when the family eats from a common platter.

2. It is a noble attitude of mind to not disdain to eat with others, poor or rich, young or old.

3. Those who have bodily defects are allowed and entitled to eat with healthy and sound people, provided there is no possibility of contagion or the defects are not of a horrifying nature.

4. Hands should be washed before and after a meal.

5. There should be no hurry to take or swallow food while it is still hot; it is better to wait until it has cooled somewhat. Breathing or blowing on food in order to cool it should be avoided.

6. On eating, a Muslim should start by saying: *Bismillāh al-Raḥmān al-Raḥīm* (In the name of Allah, the Merciful, the Mercy-giving). The following invocation may also be said: *Allāhuma bārik lanā fīma razaqtanā wa qinā 'adhāb al-nār* (O God, bless this food and protect us from Hell).

7. If a Muslim forgets to mention God's name over the food when he begins eating he should say: *Bismillāhi awwaluhū wa ākhiruhū* (In the name of God at the beginning and at the end) of the meal.

8. It is not enough that one of the group at a meal mention God's name. It is the duty of everyone present to do so.

9. Food should not be taken from all sides of the platter, but eaten from that which is nearest. If, however, the platter contains fruits or dates, then selection may be made from any side.

10. If a Muslim is served with food and the time for prayer comes, he should first have his food and not hasten to prayer until he has finished eating, provided there is no danger that the time for the prayer will elapse before

he finishes eating. The purpose of this is to help him to concentrate on his *ṣalāt*, something that cannot be achieved when thinking of food.

11. Eating should be done using the right hand only, using a spoon, or using three fingers of the right hand after washing them, if spoons are not available.

12. Food should be eaten slowly and not greedily.

13. If the person who is eating likes the food, then he may express approval and admiration, otherwise he should never be disrespectful and criticize or express disapproval of it. In the latter case he may say, 'I do not want any' or 'I am not used to this kind of food.'

14. Eating cold and hot food at the same time is not recommended as it might be harmful to the teeth and stomach.

15. Talk should be light, neither controversial nor provocative, and should avoid at all costs anything involving distasteful descriptions, for this may upset others.

16. It is bad manners to speak with a mouth full of food.

17. If some food falls from the mouth while eating, it should be cleaned, if possible, and eaten. This is because wastefulness is forbidden. This applies also to leaving large remnants of meat on the bones, which is also wasteful.

18. It is permissible to greet people engaged in eating, but is impolite to shake hands with them.

19. A Muslim should not eat a great amount of food. He should stop eating before his stomach is full. Voracious eating is an un-Islamic habit.

20. Going to sleep immediately after eating is unhealthy.

21. Unconsumed food should not be left on the plate.

22. When a Muslim has finished eating, he should praise God for the food by saying: *Alḥamdu lillāhilladhī aṭ'amanā wa saqānā wa ja'alanā muslīmīn* (Praise be to God who has given us food and drink and made us Muslims). He can also praise God by saying: *Allāhumma bārik lanā fīhi wa aṭ'imnā khayran minhu* (Praise be to God in abundance, bless us with food and give us better to eat).

23. Hands and mouth should be washed after eating.[1] Washing is especially necessary after greasy food. After the meal, a toothpick should be used to clean food remnants from teeth. This helps to maintain healthy teeth.

24. Politeness requires that children do not start eating before their parents and members of the family do not eat before guests. Respect for elders is one of the principles of Islam.

25. If a fly falls into food or drink, it should be pushed down until it is submerged and then drawn out and thrown away. The reason for this, as given in an authentic *ḥadīth*, is that every fly carries on one wing malady and on the other remedy.

26. A Muslim should try to ensure that everything he eats outside the home is *ḥalāl* (food permitted for Muslims).

27. Newspapers or correspondence should not be read at meals if this leads to spending a great deal of time over the meal.

Drinking

1. Intoxicating beverages of all kinds are forbidden.
2. Drinking out of silver or gold vessels is forbidden. Any other kind of vessel may be used.

---

1. See previous note on p. 67.

3. Drinks should be kept clean, especially water, and the containers should be covered, especially at night.

4. A vessel should be checked before drinking to make sure that nothing has fallen into it.

5. The right hand should be used for drinking, and not the left hand unless there is a necessity.

6. God's name should be mentioned upon drinking by saying: *Bismillāh al-Raḥmān al-Raḥīm* (In the name of Allah, the Merciful, the Mercy-giving).

7. Drinking directly from the mouth of a bottle, jug, waterskin or leather container should be avoided.

8. A cup with a broken edge should not be used for drinking.

9. When drinking one should not breathe into the vessel. One's thirst should not be quenched in one gulp. The cup should be removed from the mouth, a breath taken, and then a further drink.

10. If drinking from a spring, river or pool, the drinker should avoid putting his mouth to it while lying on his stomach; he should use his hands instead, after washing.

11. It is recommended to drink quietly, not gulping, from a cup or glass. In the course of drinking the vessel should be removed from the mouth and a breath taken. This should be repeated three times during the drink, dividing it into three sections. This is more thirst-quenching, healthier and wholesome.

12. One should not drink while standing, reclining or lying down. Drinking should be carried out while sitting unless there is a necessity, for instance when drinking from a water fountain.

13. When a Muslim finishes drinking, he should praise God and thank Him for it. After drinking milk, there is a special thanks: *Allāhumma bārik lanā fīhi wa zidnā minhu* (O God bless us with it and prosper us from it) for the benefit contained in the milk.

14. When a group of people drink, the one on the right should drink first, regardless of age; that is, the vessel should actually be passed to the right. One should ask permission of the one sitting on one's right to interrupt passing to the right so as to give the drink to another person.

15. When a person distributes something to drink among a group of people he should give it to whoever is on his right, then proceed along to the right, even if there is on his left an old person. Preference should always be given to those on the right. The drink should be passed with the right hand.

16. If a Muslim is offered something to drink by someone, he should not forget to thank him and pray God to bless him.

17. If something is drunk which contains fat or sugar acid, such as milk, then the mouth should be rinsed afterward in order to keep it clean and healthy.

18. A hot drink should not be blown on to cool it; it is better to wait until it has cooled.

19. If a dog drinks from a vessel, then it must be washed seven times with water, including once with clay if available, otherwise with soap. Such washing is specifically for dogs' saliva (not for other animals).

5

Dress

Though clothes are an important element in the expression of human personality and social exchange, they remain, from the point of view of Islam, only a means, and should not become an end in themselves. The purpose of clothes is primarily to cover the human body and to protect it from heat or cold.

There is no special fashion to which all members of the society should adhere. On the contrary, to adhere to one type of fashion is not according to the teachings of Islam. However, general guidelines are laid down concerning dress. Some of these guidelines are common to both sexes, others relate specifically to men's or to women's clothes.

Common Principles

1. Muslims should distinguish themselves in dress from other nations. They should also not imitate non-Muslims in their dress or in any other way.

2. A clear distinction should be observed between male and female dress. No man may dress like a woman, nor any woman like a man.

3. Wearing such clothes as demonstrate arrogance and haughtiness is forbidden. In fact, arrogance and pride in any respect are not permitted. Of course, beauty and smartness of appearance do not necessarily imply arro-

gance. It is acceptable to wish to please God and thank Him through one's appearance.

4. A man's clothes should cover his body from at least his navel to his knees. A woman's clothes should cover the whole of her body except hands and face.

5. Clothes covering the above-mentioned parts of a woman's body, or a man's body should not be diaphanous or transparent.

6. Uniforms are not forbidden: professionals (soldiers, policemen, etc.) may dress to declare their profession or job. However, the *'Ulamā'* or the scholars of Islam, should not distinguish themselves by dressing in a special uniform. Islam forbids anything that might contribute to the setting up of a clergy.

7. It is not important to wear new clothes so much as to wear clothes that are clean. Clothes should be kept clean by washing them frequently, and dirty clothes should never be worn.

8. Clothes need not be of a certain colour. The ideal colour for a Muslim's clothes is white.

9. Clothes should be worn that are easy to put on and take off.

10. When a Muslim buys new clothes, he must thank God for granting him the means to have them.

11. When putting on clothes, one should begin with the right side, and when taking them off, begin with the left side, mentioning God's name in both cases, and then hang or fold them up.

Men's Dress

1. Notice must be taken of the common guidelines of dress which have already been explained.

2. Wearing silk, brocade, embroidered silk or a garment hemmed with silk of more than four finger's breadth, is forbidden for men. Licence, however, is given for men to wear them on medical or health grounds.

3. Men should also avoid dressing in clothes dyed with saffron or with a reddish-yellow dye. There is no harm, however, in women wearing these colours.

4. Wearing clothes of a non-Islamic character constitutes a kind of imitation of other nations, which is forbidden.

5. Men's dress consists of the following:

    (a) Undershirt worn against the skin and made mainly of cotton.

    (b) Underwear to cover the lower part of the body.

    (c) Suit of clothes consisting of two pieces, a lower garment to cover the lower part of the body and an upper garment for the upper half of the body. No part of the lower garment should reach below the ankles. The sleeves of both undershirt and upper garment should not be wide nor extend below the wrist, if this is done for arrogance.

    (d) Headgear in the form of a turban or cap.

6. Sport and swimming wear. Sportswear for men should conform to the common rule for covering nakedness, the part of the body from the navel to the knees; these parts should not be exposed to others. So sports may be played in a special type of shorts which should be ample enough not to exaggerate or otherwise show the man's form.

Women's Dress

1. The common guidelines on dress should be taken note of.

2. A woman's dress must conform to several requirements simultaneously, namely:

   (a) It must cover and conceal the whole of her body except the face and hands.

   (b) The garments should not be so thin or transparent as to reveal her body.

   (c) The main garment must be a 'flowing' one, that is, the woman must avoid tight or clinging clothes which exaggerate or show her figure, or any part of it, such as breasts, legs or arms.

   (d) Muslim women, in order to safeguard their cultural identity, are discouraged from imitating the dress of non-Muslim women.

   (e) In order to maintain their feminine identity women are forbidden to imitate men in dress.

   (f) It is necessary to avoid clothes that attract the attention of others.

   (g) Wearing perfume on clothes either outdoors or when meeting strangers indoors should be avoided.

3. A Muslim woman's dress consists of three pieces: a shift, a veil and a cloak.

   (a) Shift – a garment covering the whole body except head, face and hands. It must be long enough so that the woman's feet are entirely covered. The shift should cover the whole body. Therefore, to limit it to the knees and cover the legs with long stockings is not allowed. The sleeves of the shift should not be wide.

   (b) Veil – the head-dress, is a covering to protect and conceal the woman's head and neck. It cannot be of fine net but may be made of any other material. It also cannot be of transparent material unless the folds make it opaque.

(c) Cloak – a garment to enwrap the body, rests on the top of the head and the shoulders. This helps to conceal the size of the woman's head and shoulders.

Shoes

1. Shoes designed or made to be used by men may not be used by women, and vice versa.
2. New shoes should be bought as often as needed, if the buyer is financially able, provided that this is done without extravagance and that the purpose of doing so is not arrogance.
3. Shoes should be kept tidy and clean, though they should not receive excessive attention.
4. The right shoe should be put on first, and when taking them off, the left one first, mentioning God's name in both cases.
5. When putting on shoes, they should be checked to ensure that no harmful insect has hidden in them during the night or while they have not been in use.
6. When taking off shoes, they should be placed where they are not likely to disturb others through any unpleasant odour.

6

Architecture and Furniture

The Muslim Dwelling

1. A dwelling is one of the most important necessities of life. The fact that it is essential does not mean that a Muslim should spend large sums of money on building beautiful houses, concerning himself with matters of secondary importance, such as ornamentation and unnecessary rooms. The sole purpose of the dwelling should be to protect the occupant from extremes of weather and to guarantee needed privacy.

2. It is essential that bedrooms should be of two kinds, separated from one another; one for the parents, the other for the children. Girls and boys should sleep apart from the age of ten.

3. Since Muslim women are not allowed to bathe in common baths, the dwelling must contain a room for bathing.

4. It is preferable to have the lavatory separate from the bathroom.

Furniture

1. The main characteristics of furniture in the Muslim dwelling are simplicity and necessity. Indulging in a luxurious life has, in fact, serious effects on the morals and behaviour of individuals, and of the nation as a whole.

2. Furniture should be of moderate price.

3. Curtains should be restricted to the size of the windows, in order to avoid unnecessary expenditure.

4. Silver or gold should not be used in the house, neither for furniture nor for table utensils, nor in any other articles.

5. The Muslim dwelling should be clean of images, representations of anything possessing a soul. Representation of living creatures in general is forbidden in Islam.

6. Making representations or pictures of anything such as a tree which does not possess a spirit, is permitted.

7. If there is no alternative but to use vessels belonging to or having belonged to non-Muslims, then they must be adequately cleaned.

8. Dogs are not allowed in the dwellings. Having a dog is unlawful unless it is owned for the purpose of guarding or hunting. Even in these two cases dogs should not be allowed to enter the dwelling.

Cleaning the Dwelling

1. The cleanliness and pleasant smell of the house are matters of great importance.

2. Refuse and garbage should be kept outside the house, so that bad smells will not disturb the residents and visitors.

3. Attention should be paid to the cleanliness of the courtyard, its entrance and the garden.
4. Muslims should not be influenced by non-Islamic beliefs, such as for example, that sweeping the house at night might harm the *jinn* or lead to poverty, or that sweeping the house following the departure on a journey of a member of the family might harm him.

Decoration and Beauty

By following and implementing the general principles of Islamic conduct, especially the principle of beauty, cleanliness and moderation in expense, the characteristics of the Muslim dwelling can be imagined – tidiness, cleanliness, simplicity, a pleasant odour, modesty.

Precautionary Measures For Safety at Home

Islam recommends the following before going to bed:

1. All doors are closed.
2. Food pots and drinking vessels are covered.
3. All sources of fire, such as gas cookers, etc. are turned off.

7

Conduct Within the Family

In Islam, the family is recognized and dignified as the basis of society. Great value is thus attached to keeping family relationships healthy and harmonious: the rules of conduct governing these relationships are of the highest importance.

Husband-Wife Relationship

How a Wife Should be Treated

1. In the view of Islam, the best man is he who is best and kindest to his wife. Acting kindly towards one's wife is an Islamic conduct.

2. A man's work life should not be pursued with such all-consuming singlemindedness that he runs the risk of destroying his marriage. Regardless of how much he must work to provide for his family, the wife nevertheless has a right to part of her husband's time. This may be spent in entertainments, enjoying each other's company, playing sports or any other pastime permitted by Islam.

3. It is part of a husband's kindness toward his wife to fulfil her needs, as long as they do not contradict Islam.

In fact, the best way to spend money, in the view of Islam, is to support one's family.

4. Though the house is better than the mosque for women to pray in, a wife should not be prevented from attending the mosque when she wishes to do so.

5. To talk to others about private affairs, namely sexual matters, is something completely forbidden in Islam.

6. A husband's jealousy of his wife is of two kinds: baseless suspicion or jealousy without reason, which is to be avoided, and jealousy where there is a good reason, which is recommended.

7. A husband should not hate his wife, for if he dislikes one of her characteristics, he may be pleased with another. It is, incidentally, forbidden in Islam to try to change those characteristics of a wife which a husband does not like, as long as these characteristics do not contradict Islam. A wife has her own personality, different from a husband's, and he has no right to try to destroy it and make it conform to his own. The husband should note that just as certain elements of his wife's character may be displeasing to him, likewise certain aspects of his own may be displeasing to her.

8. A husband should never revile his wife or her relatives.

9. The husband-wife relationship is of a special nature. It cannot be fruitful unless the couple try to overcome artificial barriers caused by shyness and social inhibitions.

10. The right given to the husband to lead the family should not result in the misuse and abuse of his authority. Therefore, he should not ask his wife for things that are beyond her capacity or give her too many orders.

11. For a husband to honour and respect his wife's close relatives will result in strengthening the relationship with his wife.

12. To honour, respect and be hospitable to his wife's friends and relations is in fact a mark of respect for her.

13. As mentioned in Chapter 12, the most necessary conditions to be fulfilled in the marriage are those contained in the marriage contract, so after marriage care must be taken not to neglect or forget them, providing that they are in accordance with Islamic law.

14. To dwell on and count a wife's mistakes, to disapprove of her deeds, and to blame her frequently will endanger a marriage. Husbands are advised to ignore their wife's mistakes in many cases.

15. A husband's and father's indifference to his wife or children violating the orders of Islam is a grave mistake that a Muslim should not dare to make.

16. For a husband to blame his wife or disapprove of her acts in the presence of others, such as their children, relatives, etc., is rude conduct.

17. A husband is not allowed to ask his wife to work to earn money. To support her is the responsibility of the husband alone.

18. On returning home, a husband should not enter the house without first telling his family of his arrival by ringing the bell or knocking on the door. He should signal his arrival by mentioning God's name in praise, greet them, pray two *rak'ahs* and then ask them how they are.

19. A husband should try to keep the odour of his mouth pleasant, so that his wife may not be offended or displeased.

20. A husband's relationship with his wife should be characterized by a balance between resoluteness without harshness and flexibility without weakness.

Correct Conduct of a Muslim Wife

1. To be a good wife is so important that from the viewpoint of Islam, a good wife is considered to be the best thing in the world.

2. The role of the wife in the marriage is extremely important, indeed it is the decisive factor.

3. Wives must do their best to keep their husbands pleased with them.

4. The ideal wife combines three merits: she pleases her husband when he sees her, by taking care to appear beautiful before him; she obeys him when he gives a command; she does not go against his wishes regarding her person or property by doing anything of which he disapproves.

5. To refuse to go with her husband when he calls her to bed is a grave mistake that a wife must avoid.

6. When a wife intends to fast voluntarily, she may do so only with her husband's permission. If she does not receive his permission, then he has the right to make her break her fast when she is observing it. The reason for this is that he might wish to have sex with her, which he cannot do if she is fasting with his permission.

7. It is a wife's duty not to allow anyone, that her husband does not want, to enter the house without his permission.

8. A wife may not give anything away of her husband's property without his permission.

9. A wife should avoid asking a husband for extra money, or for that which he does not possess and cannot provide, and she should show gratitude for whatever is given.

10. A wife should acknowledge any assistance given in the house by her husband.

11. A good wife is one who is true to her husband's word if he adjures her to do something.

12. On a husband's return home, a wife should receive him kindly and meet him with a good and beautiful appearance.

13. A wife should try not to neglect her husband's needs or ignore his demands. The more a wife takes care of her husband, the more she will be loved. Most husbands, in fact, consider their wives' care for them as an expression of their love.

14. A wife should be careful not to offer to her husband, on his coming home, the family problems, or to complain to him about the children, etc. Instead, she should try to create the peaceful atmosphere that her husband needs after a long and tiring day.

15. A wife should discuss family problems with her husband at appropriate times.

16. For a wife to hold her husband's close relatives in respect and treat them kindly is, in fact, a mark of respect and honour for the husband.

17. Leaving the house excessively is a bad habit for a woman. She should also not leave the house if her husband objects to her doing so.

18. A wife must not converse with strange men against her husband's objections.

19. A wife should be attentive to her husband when he speaks.

20. A wife does not have the right to lend anything of her husband's property against his wishes. However, she can lend from her own property.

21. Asking a husband for a divorce without a strong reason is forbidden.

22. If a husband's friends inquire about him, a wife should answer them but without indulging in lengthy conversation.

23. Too many arguments and disputes with a husband, heaping abuse on him, leads, in fact, to hatred and a deterioration of the relationship.

24. Taking care of the house and running the household are the wife's responsibility. Therefore, she should carry out duties in keeping the house, furniture, etc., and be frugal.

25. A wife may not give alms from her husband's property without his permission.

26. Speaking to or telling others about sexual matters between a husband and wife is a grave sin in Islam.

27. A wife should not be afraid to express her love and affection for her husband. It will please him and bind him closer to the family; moreover, if he does not find an attractive, loving woman at home, he may be driven for solace elsewhere, outside the home.

28. Leadership in the family is given to the husband. For the wife to demand complete and full equality with her husband will result in having two masters in the family and this does not exist in Islam. However, the husband should not behave in an autocratic manner and misuse his position. He should display love and affection and treat his wife as a partner in life.

Parents' Conduct Toward Their Children

1. Children are usually the joy of one's life as well as a source of pride. Therefore, parents should avoid indulg-

ing in over-confidence, false pride, and be on guard against misdeeds which might arise out of love for their children.

2. The child's dependence on the parents makes their role in the formation of the child's personality a decisive one.

3. The three most inalienable rights of the child in Islam are: the right to life and equal chances in life, the right of legitimacy which holds that every child shall have a legal father, a good upbringing and general care.

4. Interest in and the responsibility for the child's welfare are questions of first priority to the parents.

5. As mentioned in Chapter 13, by the time the child is seven days old, it is recommended that (a) the child be given a good, pleasant name; (b) its head be shaved; (c) a sheep be sacrificed for a baby girl and two for a baby boy[1] and the meat shared with relatives, friends and the poor. The whole ceremony is known as *'aqīqah*.

6. A father can give his children nothing better than a good education. The most necessary education that he should provide his children with is Islamic education, especially in the Qur'ān and the *Sunnah*.

7. The best of mothers, in the view of Islam, are those who are the most affectionate to their small children.

8. Male children should never be preferred over female or vice versa. However, Islam stresses the importance of taking special care of daughters, treating them nicely, and showing them kindness.

9. Fathers, if able, should help their sons and daughters to marry when they reach puberty.

---

1. This is perhaps because the law of inheritance grants one share to a daughter and two shares to a son.

10. To be fond of children and kind to them is a good quality. In fact, the Muslim society should be noted among other communities for its kindness to children.

11. Whether the parents are alive or deceased, present or absent, known or unknown, the child must be provided for with the best care, either by relatives or the state.

12. For parents, establishing full justice in all aspects of dealing with their children is of great importance.

13. For parents to show affection for their children by embracing and kissing them is good conduct.

14. Parents must avoid overprotectiveness as well as negligence in bringing up their children.

15. Parents must ask their children only to do things according to their capability and must not put heavy burdens upon them. Abuse of parental authority is a bad thing.

16. Parents should accept their children's gifts with appreciation, even though the gifts may be small.

17. Bringing up children according to the teachings of Islam is extremely important. Training them in religious life from a very early age is necessary. When they reach the age of seven, parents should make sure that they begin praying.

18. Educating children concerning Islamic conduct and the various aspects of Islam is the parents' responsibility.

19. Children's obedience to parents depends to a certain extent upon the parents. Being over-demanding and asking too much of them might lead to disobedience.

20. From the age of ten, girls and boys should sleep apart.

21. It is not permissible for a mother, sister or daughter to expose her body to a grown-up son, brother or father,

except: (a) head and face; (b) neck and collar area; (c) from the mid-upper arm to the fingertips; and (d) lower part of the feet.

Children's Conduct Toward Their Parents

The following directions should govern a child's, even a grown-up child's, relationship with his parents:

1. The special relationship between children and parents imposes a heavy responsibility on children towards their parents. There are none who better deserve a child's kindness, patience and good manners than his parents.

2. Parents are much more sensitive to any act of discourtesy toward them from their own children than from any others, thus children are advised to be especially considerate when dealing with their parents.

3. Parents usually believe that they are more experienced, wise and right, even though they might be wrong. This belief sustains their feeling that they are a child's guardians even after the child has grown up. This attitude must be met with great understanding and patience.

4. Though both parents deserve a child's kindness, the most deserving of friendly care from a child is his mother, and then his father. According to the Prophet: 'Paradise is at your mother's feet.'

5. It is impolite conduct for a child to call his parents by their first name.

6. One of the finest acts of kindness is to respect a father's friends and to treat them in a kind way even after he has died.

7. Children are responsible for the support and maintenance of their parents. It is an absolute religious duty to provide for parents in case of need and to help make their lives as comfortable as possible.

8. A child should try to avoid anything that might irritate his parents. One of a child's duties toward his parents entails patience and compassion. Even if parents ask a child for something that is beyond his capacity, it is his duty to apologize in a polite manner for not being able to fulfil their wish.

9. A man's relationship with his parents and his wife should not be at the expense of each other, nor should one be sacrificed for the other. Both should be characterized by harmony and reconciliation.

10. When a child speaks to his parents, he should speak politely and gently.

11. If obedience and loyalty to his parents is likely to alienate the individual from God, he must side with God. It is true that parents should expect obedience from their children, but if their actions intrude upon the rights of God, a demarcation line must be drawn and maintained. In this case, to refuse to carry out their orders is obligatory provided that it is done in a polite and proper way.

12. Being patient, grateful, compassionate, respectful and affectionate toward parents is a necessity even if they are idolaters and ill-disposed toward Islam.

13. Providing parents with sincere counsel is required of a child.

14. It is a child's duty to listen well to his parents when they speak to him. He should never interrupt his parents while they are speaking and never argue with them.

15. When accompanying one parent outdoors a child should not walk in front of him/her while walking, and not take a seat before he/she has.

16. No child may become the cause of harm to his parents.

17. Asking a father for extra money, for what he does not possess or for what he cannot give easily, must be avoided.

18. For a child to draw attention to his own generosity toward or support of his parents is forbidden.

19. To be humble to his parents and to be of service to them in the house and outside is a great honour, whatever a child's position is.

20. It is a child's duty to take care of his parents when they get old by having them live with him in his house. To get rid of them by sending them to a home for the aged is considered not only discourteous but also obnoxious.

21. If meeting others with a smiling face is considered an act of kindness by someone, it is considered, in the case of a child meeting his parents, a necessity.

22. A child should take the initiative and greet his parents when he meets them. He should not expect that his father or mother would greet him first.

23. A child is supposed to respect and treat his parents kindly even if they disregard and treat him wrongfully.

24. To revile parents is one of the most serious sins. A child should also avoid reviling someone else's parents, lest they should revile his.

25. However much a child is in disagreement with one of his parents, he should not say a cross word or make a gesture that would hurt him or her.

26. A foster mother is one of his relatives, so a child must not neglect his duties toward her.

27. Still other types of kindness are due to parents after their death, such as prayers for them, asking forgiveness for them, honouring their legitimate commitments and honouring their friends.

28. Getting old causes parents to grow physically weak and mentally feeble. This is often accompanied by impatience, degeneration of energy, heightened sensitivity and, perhaps, misjudgement. Therefore, it is a child's duty to take cognizance of that fact when it occurs and increase his patience and kindness to his elderly parents.

29. It is the duty of children to help their parents with the household work without having to be asked to do so.

30. Disobedience, neglect, unkindness toward parents are considered as sins. All mistakes in life can perhaps be understood and explained away but not those committed against parents.

8
Reading and Reciting the Qur'ān

1. The best Muslims are those who learn and teach the Qur'ān. Knowledge of the Qur'ān and reciting it are two merits.

2. The Qur'ān should be held, taken or given with the right hand not the left.

3. Women during child-bed or during the menstrual cycle and men and women who are seminally defiled, may neither touch nor read the Qur'ān.

4. All chapters of the Qur'ān and all of its words are benevolent and beneficial.

5. Gathering in a group to read and study the Qur'ān is recommended.

6. Listening carefully while the Qur'ān is being recited or read is not only an act of politeness, but an obligatory duty upon every Muslim.

7. Reading the Qur'ān with proper contemplation, thinking and concentration is necessary to understand the meaning fully.

8. The Qur'ān is a book of guidance. It is not a book of history, science, geography, etc., in spite of the fact

that it contains historical, scientific, geographical and various other facts.

9. The Qur'ān is a book of guidance for mankind in every respect of life. It is not meant to be recited only at ceremonial openings and such occasions.

10. When buying or selling the Qur'ān and no fixed price is attached, using terms and tones of language usually used when bargaining should be avoided.

11. A Muslim's knowledge of the Qur'ān should be refreshed by re-reading it frequently; this applies especially to those who memorize it, for it is difficult to remember it when it is abandoned for a while.

12. When reading or reciting the Qur'ān, the established rules of pronunciation and intonation included in an independent science called *al-tajwīd* should be followed; these rules have been passed down from the time of the Prophet and the Companions.

13. When reciting the Qur'ān, it should be beautified with a good voice and the verses chanted, not sung, for a beautiful voice increases the beauty of the Qur'ān. This however should not be done in a way contradicting the rules of *al-tajwīd*. The inclination of some, to recite the Qur'ān with a melodious voice approaching singing, thus contradicting the rules of *al-tajwīd*, is forbidden. The listener should take the first opportunity to correct such a recitation and politely draw attention to its incorrectness.

14. When reciting one of the fourteen special verses of the Qur'ān requiring prostration upon completion of the verse, the Qur'ān should be laid aside, and a *sajdah* (a prostration) made.

15. A Muslim should not be hasty to judge others' reciting of the Qur'ān.

16. Disputing, arguing or engaging in controversy about the Qur'ān must not be indulged in, for it is the Book of God.

9

The Mosque

The mosque is where Muslims should pray five times every day, where they seek refuge from the troubles of this world, from its everlasting daily demands, its complications and its vanities.

Design

1. A mosque should be built in every residential district.//

2. The design of the mosque should be characterized by simplicity, as must its furnishings.

3. The mosque should be devoid of any lavish kind of ornamentation, representation of anything, pictures or images.

4. Extravagance in spending large sums of money to build luxurious mosques should be avoided.

5. Members of the Muslim society should neither vie with one another about the virtues or beauties of any particular mosque nor compete in building ostentatious mosques.

6. Attaching pieces of gold or silver to any part of the mosque or its furnishings is forbidden.

7. The carpets and walls of the mosque should be devoid of a multiplicity of colours for that distracts the concentration of the worshippers.

8. Writing on the walls of the mosque, inside or outside, including Qur'ānic verses or God's attributes, should be avoided. The names of the Prophet and the first four rightly-guided caliphs likewise should not be written.

9. The *minbar* should not be placed in the middle of the mosque. Its height should not exceed three steps.

10. Every mosque should have two entrances, one for men and one for women.

11. Lavatories should be sited as far from the mosque as practicable, and from the fountains or basins for ritual ablution.

12. Raising flags inside the mosque is an innovation.

Cleanliness and Tidiness

The mosque deserves to be the cleanest place on earth. Therefore:

1. Muslims must be sure before entering the mosque that their body and clothes are clean and do not smell bad.

2. Filth must be removed from shoes and the shoes removed before entering the mosque.

3. Although it is not forbidden to eat anything in the mosque, it is not a place for taking meals and drinks.

4. Whoever brings in or causes dirt in the mosque has a duty to clean it up and remove it. It is not the duty solely of the mosque caretaker to keep the mosque clean and tidy; it is also the responsibility of every Muslim entering the mosque and seeing any uncleanliness, to remove this from the mosque.

5. The mosque should be sprayed or sprinkled with perfume to give a pleasant odour.

10

Behaviour on Fridays

1. Though Friday, according to Islam, is the best day on which the sun has ever risen, and the lord of days, it is not the Islamic sabbath, because sabbath does not exist in Islam.

2. A Muslim should bathe or purify himself with *wuḍū'* as perfectly as possible before going to prayer. Though bathing is not obligatory, it has a more cleansing effect; though *wuḍū'* is good, bathing is more excellent.

3. Best clothes should be worn and perfume applied, if this is available, or pleasant-smelling oil should be put on the hair.

4. A toothstick or toothbrush should be used to ensure that the mouth is clean and has a pleasant odour. This is more important on Fridays before leaving for prayer than on other days.

5. Before leaving for prayer, nails should be cut and cleaned, and one should ensure that clothes are clean and beard and moustache tidy.

6. The Friday prayer in congregation is a necessary duty for every Muslim, with certain exceptions, e.g. children, women, invalids and those too ill to perform prayer.

7. If there is more than one mosque available, it is yet better to say the Friday prayer together at one mosque.

8. Going as early as possible to the mosque on Friday is recommended. Walking to the mosque, if this is possible, and not riding is also more worthy.

9. On entering the mosque, the rules of behaviour in the mosque as discussed in Chapter 16, must be observed.

10. Care should be taken to avoid annoying others in the mosque; for example, squeezing between two men or stepping on others.

11. Most mosques on Fridays become full of worshippers. No individual has the right to make another get up and then move into his place. He should politely ask those present to make room for him.

12. While in the mosque, the worshipper must avoid any sitting position which could cause him to drowse, to sleep, or which would invalidate his *wuḍū'*.

13. If a worshipper should find himself dozing, he should try to change his place. In this case, he should change places with his neighbour.

14. A worshipper should avoid taking any position that would uncover his body between the navel and the knees.

15. The Prophet Muhammad forbade worshippers to sit together in a circle in the mosque before Friday prayer, because this hinders straight rows, and reduces the available space.

16. Facing the *imām* while he is giving *khuṭbah* from the *minbar* (pulpit) is polite conduct.

17. When the *imām* asks God's blessings, etc. for the Muslims, he should not raise his hands in an attitude of supplication.

18. When the Friday prayer is finished worshippers should not rush to leave the mosque, or crowd the exits.

19. As mentioned above, a sabbath does not exist in Islam, therefore, it is not required that a Muslim abandons working during the whole of Friday. What is required, is to stop working during prayer time.

20. A worshipper should listen to the *imām* as soon as he starts his *khuṭbah* and keep silent until he finishes. To attend prayer with a frivolous attitude is against the aim of the Friday prayer.

21. It is undesirable to fast on Friday alone; to fast on Friday, however, in conjunction with Thursday or Saturday is allowed.

22. It is neither necessary nor required to abandon travel on Friday.

23. Friday is a good occasion to remember the Prophet, peace be on him, and invoke a blessing on him by saying: *Allāhuma Ṣalli 'alā Muḥammad wa 'alā āli Muḥammad* (O God, bless Muḥammad and Muḥammad's family).

24. Reading the Qur'ānic chapter of *Al-Kahf* every Friday is recommended.

Khuṭbah at Friday Prayer

1. The *imām* should avoid the custom of always wearing black clothes on Fridays.

2. As soon as the *imām* ascends the *minbar* he salutes the worshippers, just before he sits or immediately after.

3. The *imām* should face the worshippers while he is delivering the *khuṭbah*.

4. Topics discussed in the *khuṭbah* should be related to current, relevant issues.

5. The Friday *khuṭbah* is of two parts in each of which the *imām* must speak while standing; in the interval between he must sit for a short while on the *minbar*.

6. The voice of the *imām* should be clear, but he should not shout in order to be heard. His language should be simple and understandable.

7. The *imām* should not interrupt his *khuṭbah* in order to greet someone or to make an announcement of any kind.

8. The *imām* should not make his *khuṭbah* or his prayer lengthy. Each must be of moderate length. In fact, the shortness of the *khuṭbah* is a sign of the *imām*'s understanding and knowledge of Islam.

9. The second part of the *khuṭbah* should not be devoid of information.

10. The *khuṭbah* is a message and not a performance. The *imām* should avoid being conspicuously eloquent or poetic; he should also avoid speaking in a voice or in a manner which tends towards musicality.

11. The *imām*'s raising his hands in the *khuṭbah* while saying *du'ā'*[1] for the Muslims is not recommended. It is enough that he points with his forefinger.

12. The *imām* should prepare his *khuṭbah* beforehand; his *du'ā'* should preferably be spontaneous and not memorized.

13. The *imām* should not begin the actual prayer until he has convinced himself that the rows of worshippers are straight.

---

1. *Du'ā'* is a prayer of invocation, calling for blessings from God or for protection from evil.

11

Celebrating the Feasts

Feasts in Islam are confined to two occasions: *'Īd al-Fiṭr* (Feast at end of Fast) which immediately follows the month of Ramaḍān, and *'Īd al-Aḍḥā* (Feast of Sacrifice) which falls on the tenth day of the month of pilgrimage (*Dhu'l-Hijja*). Both are occasions to thank God for having allowed individual and community to fulfil their religious duty.

Observing the Feasts

1. Taking a bath on the occasion of the two Feasts is recommended. This can be done any time after midnight preceding the Feast day.

2. A Muslim should dress well and wear a pleasant perfume before leaving for the Feast prayers.

3. Before going to pray in the morning on the day of *'Īd al-Fiṭr,* eating some dates, or sweets, is recommended.

4. It is preferable not to eat anything on the day of *'Īd al-Aḍḥā* until performing the Feast prayer in the morning; then one should return home, slaughter an animal, and prepare the Feast meal.

5. Walking to the place of the Feast prayer is recommended unless it is too far away to do so.

6. The Feast congregational prayer is usually not performed in the mosque, unless it is raining. To perform it in an open square is recommended.

7. It is recommended that the whole Muslim community, with the exception of invalids and the disabled, should gather in the open square for the Feast prayer. This includes menstruating women, who may be present at the occasion but who may not participate in the prayer.

8. It is strongly recommended to wait and listen to the Feast *khuṭbah* given by the *imām*.

9. When going back to his home after the prayer a Muslim should return by a different road from the one he took when going to the prayer. This will provide him with an opportunity to meet a larger number of Muslims than would otherwise be the case.

10. One should take the initiative and congratulate Muslims on this occasion by saying: *Taqabbal Allāh minnā wa minkum* (May God accept the work we have done for His sake).

11. The rules of conduct and behaviour in the mosque, discussed in Chapter 16, must be followed here as well.

12. Fasting on the day of *'Īd al-Fiṭr* or during the three days following the day of *'Īd al-Aḍḥā* is forbidden.

13. A Muslim should dress his children beautifully, buy them sweets, and help them to celebrate and experience the occasion. This is necessary to help them identify with their Islamic culture.

14. A Muslim must avoid doing anything that would annoy his family or dampen their good spirits and spoil their good humour on this occasion.

15. Fathers and responsible persons should ensure on such occasions that Islamic law is adhered to, as these Feasts are to thank God and not to indulge in disobedience to Him. Thus, such things as mixing of the sexes, etc. should not occur, although such happy occasions could easily give rise to the wish to do so.

Behaviour on 'Īd al-Aḍḥā

'Īd al-Aḍḥā lasts two days after the day of sacrifice, which falls on the tenth day of the lunar Islamic month of *Dhu'l-Hijjah*.

1. It is obligatory, whether one is a pilgrim or not, that every family who is *Ṣāḥib niṣāb* (one liable for *Zakāt*), offer a sacrifice on this occasion. By sacrifice is meant the slaughtering of certain kinds of animals.

2. The sacrificial animal should be chosen from healthy stock. An animal whose ear or tongue has been clipped, whose horns have been broken, or who is crippled, should not be selected; the animal should be more than one year old; if sheep, goat, cow or ox, more than two years; and if camel or she-camel, more than five years.

3. The sacrificial animal is irreplaceable by alms equal to the cost of the animal.

4. The sacrifice may be a sheep, a goat, a cow, or a camel. A cow or a camel serves for seven people, who share with one another the sacrifice.

5. The correct time for slaughtering is upon return from the Feast prayer. Therefore, slaughtering should be avoided before that time, since that will not be considered a sacrifice. If one sacrifice is made before the prayer, another sacrifice may be made after the prayer.

6. If a person can slaughter well, then it is recommended that he performs the slaughtering himself, otherwise he should entrust someone to slaughter on his behalf.

7. When slaughtering the sacrifice the knife must be sharp, the animal must face towards the Ka'bah and God's name must be mentioned, saying: *Bismillāh, Allāh Akbar* (In the name of Allah, Allah is most Great).

8. A sacrifice may be slaughtered at home, though it is preferable, if possible, to perform the slaughtering in the open square where the prayer was performed.

9. Parts of the animal may be eaten or kept by the person making the sacrifice. A large part of it, however, should be given to the poor. Something may also be given to the relatives of the person making the sacrifice.

10. The time of slaughtering sacrifices lasts four days including the first day of the feast.[1]

11. Selling any part of the sacrificial animal or giving any part of it, including the hide, to the butcher or person who slaughtered it, in payment, is forbidden.

Special Instructions for 'Īd al-Fiṭr

1. *Zakāt* or *ṣadaqah al-Fiṭr*[2] must be given by every financially able Muslim on the occasion of breaking the fast of the month of Ramaḍān.

2. *Zakāt al-Fiṭr* should also be given for those who are supported by a Muslim, such as his wife and children.

3. Giving the above-mentioned alms to the poor must be done before the Muslims go out to pray the Feast prayer. This will enable the poor to participate in the festival. However, if one forgets to pay *Zakāt al-Fiṭr* before the prayer, it must be paid as soon as possible afterwards.

---

1. According to Imām Abū Ḥanīfa, it is limited to three days.
2. Special alms of a certain amount, the equivalent of two meals. It should be given to the poor on behalf of each member of the family.

12

Marriage

Marriage is an important social institution which perfects the human personality. Every young man able to support a wife and family should marry, for marriage preserves one from immorality. Living in celibacy is an act abhorred in Islam. Moreover, there is nothing like marriage for increasing the love of two people.

Those who cannot marry for financial reasons are advised to fast from time to time, for fasting is a means of suppressing sexual desire. If a Muslim has no desire for marriage, or does not need it, even though he is financially able to support a family, then he should not marry.

The Search For a Wife

1. A man cannot marry a woman who is *mahram* according to the Islamic law. Seven classes of women are prohibited by reason of consanguinity and seven by reason of relationship by marriage.

2. The woman who most adheres to Islam is the ideal wife. A woman may be married for her property, her rank, or her beauty. These foundations of marriage, however, never last and can unbalance the relationship between the couple. Therefore, there must be common ground to enable understanding and to overcome misunderstanding, and that ground is adherence to Islam.

3. A decorous shyness and sensitivity are other attributes required in a wife.

4. Satisfaction with moderate material demands, with life at a moderate and not lavish standard, is a good quality in a wife. Waste of money is an indication of an irresponsible wife.

5. Marriage with a non-relative enlarges the circle of relatives by adding new ones.

6. One should avoid marriage with an infertile woman, and marry a woman who is fertile, for children are an important element in a successful marriage.

7. There is nothing at all wrong in marrying a divorced woman provided that she does not wish to return to her first husband.

8. Marriage to a virgin is preferred to marriage to a woman who has been married previously, though there is nothing wrong in marrying the latter.

9. A man should not ask a woman to marry him unless he has enough knowledge about the degree of her adherence to Islam, her background represented by the life of her parents, and other necessary information.

10. It is necessary for a man to see the woman he intends to marry, and for a woman to see the man she intends to marry.

11. Meeting the woman a man plans to marry is allowed only in the presence of a *mahram*, with whom marriage is forbidden.

12. The parts of the woman's body allowed to be seen by the man are her face and hands. The face can give an idea of her beauty and the hands can give some idea of the size of her figure.

The Woman's Right and Responsibility in Choosing a Husband

A woman should exercise her right to approve or disapprove of marriage to a particular man, but should be far-sighted and wise in making such a decision. Wealth, rank, good position and job, or any other material privilege, do not alone add up to proper attributes for a future husband.

The Engagement

1. Marriage and having a family are responsibilities which must be taken seriously.

2. Asking for a woman's hand in marriage while she is in her *'iddah*[1] is un-Islamic conduct.

3. Asking for a woman's hand in marriage when another man has done so already is impolite, and must be avoided. One is allowed to do so only if the other has relinquished her.

4. The woman's guardian has no right at all to make the marriage decision. The only one who has the full right to accept marriage is the woman herself, free from any kind of pressure.[2]

5. The woman, therefore, should be consulted in matters concerning herself. If she is an orphan or a virgin and says nothing, out of modesty, that indicates her consent, but if she is divorced or widowed then silence is not considered an answer. In either case, if the woman refuses, the authority of the guardian cannot be exercised against her will.

6. It is not appropriate to ask a woman directly for her hand; this should be done through the guardian.

---

[1]. Legally prescribed period of waiting during which a woman may not remarry after being widowed or divorced.

[2]. According to the Mālikī school a *bākirah*, virgin, girl cannot get married without the consent of her *walī*, guardian.

The Marriage Contract

1. The best and most worthy conditions ever fulfilled are those included in the marriage contract.[3]

2. The marriage contract cannot be written without the presence of the woman's guardian and two Muslim witnesses.

3. It is necessary that the couple intend to have a lasting marriage and not a temporary one, which is forbidden in Islam.

4. The ideal and most blessed marriage is that which involves the least burden upon the bridegroom.

5. The dowry is an important element in marriage. The man should have something to give his bride as a dowry, whatever its value may be. However, he should not be extravagant and go beyond his means in fixing the amount of dowry.

6. Going to the extreme in giving a woman her dowry is bad behaviour which could lead to a woman attaching too much importance to the size of the dowry.

7. It is prohibited for a man to give his daughter or sister in marriage on the condition that the other man gives his daughter or sister to him in marriage, without any dowry being paid by either. In other words, every marriage contract must be independent of every other marriage contract.

8. The wife's guardian must be male and a Muslim. A woman may not give a woman in marriage, nor can she give herself in marriage without a guardian.

9. The Muslim judge or *imām* is the guardian of a woman who has no guardian at all, or has a guardian who is not

---

[3]. Abstract from authentic prophetic tradition.

a Muslim, i.e. he may have been recognized by non-Islamic jurisprudence, but not by Islamic.

10. Agreement by both the man and the woman is an essential condition of Islamic marriage.

The Wedding Party

1. It is not an Islamic tradition to marry secretly without celebrating the marriage. Making the marriage publicly known is recommended in Islam.

2. Amusements are allowed at the wedding occasion. Although normally forbidden in Islam, singing is allowed on the occasion of marriage. It would be correct to send someone along with the bride to sing, when she is being escorted to her husband. But the content of the songs must not be obscene nor the singing disturb the neighbours.

3. Asking the bridegroom for unnecessary expenses at the wedding party might cause financial difficulty for the new couple and is considered as non-Islamic behaviour.

4. Those participating in *hajj* (pilgrimage) or *'umrah*[4] are not allowed to marry or to arrange marriages for others.

Conjugal Relations

1. The honeymoon does not exist in Islam and is therefore an alien tradition.

2. It is recommended that friends and relatives refrain from frequent visits to the couple during the first days of marriage.

3. Subtlety, gentleness and kindness are the most essential elements in the love-making process.

---

4. *'Umrah* is a pilgrimage to Makkah but unlike *hajj*, need not be performed at a particular time of the year and its performance is not obligatory and involves fewer ceremonies.

4. To have a pleasant odour and clean bodies at the time of love-making is necessary for both husband and wife.

5. The husband should approach his wife in a gentle manner and so avoid creating any barriers between the two.

6. The husband should place his hand on his wife's forehead and ask God's blessing on her by saying: 'O God, I ask You for the good in her and in the disposition You have given her, and I seek refuge in You from the evil in her and in the disposition You have given her.'

7. It is recommended that husband and wife pray two *rak'ahs* together before making love.

8. Making love in any position is permitted provided that intercourse is done through the vagina; the anus must be avoided.

9. If the husband has intercourse with his wife and wishes to repeat it, he would do well to perform *wuḍū'* between the two acts.

10. To sleep after love-making, without bathing, is allowed, though it is better to perform *wuḍū'* or bathe.

11. Having intercourse with a wife while she is menstruating is forbidden. If such a violation is committed, then it is required to give half a golden dinar in alms. A husband can, however, do everything with his menstruating wife except have sexual intercourse.

12. Love-making can be resumed only when a wife's monthly period comes to its end and she has thoroughly cleaned and perfumed herself or taken a bath.

Advice for Men

1. A wife has the right to have sexual intercourse with her husband from time to time, so a husband should not neglect this duty toward her.

2. For a husband to be rude and rough toward his wife during the day hours does not create an atmosphere for love-making in the evening or at night; in this case he should avoid love-making.
3. The husband should avoid taking medicines or preparations which might weaken or artificially incite his sexual desire.
4. Too much love-making can sometimes be harmful. Moderation is recommended.
5. A man should keep his body clean and pleasant smelling.

Advice for Women

1. A woman should never refuse her husband's request to go to bed, whether this request is expressed directly or indirectly, unless she is either fasting in Ramaḍān, menstruating, in child-bed or physically unfit.
2. If a wife intends to fast voluntarily, then it is her duty to get permission from her husband to do so. If he refuses permission, she may not fast. The reason for this is that her husband may want to make love.
3. For a wife to leave the initiative in playing and flattering to her husband, and take a negative attitude toward the act of love can result in disappointing her husband and have serious repercussions for the marriage.
4. A wife should keep herself tidy, clean, perfumed and as beautiful as she can before her husband at home.

The Wedding Feast

On the day following the marriage day, the husband should visit his relatives who visited him previously, thank them, ask

God's blessings for them, and invite them to a wedding feast, known as *walīmah*.

1. Holding a wedding feast, even if only with simple refreshments, is an important Islamic tradition. Rejection of the invitation is not allowed, unless the feast is of an un-Islamic nature. Those invited should accept and attend.

2. It is *sunnah* to have a wedding feast after and not before consummation of the marriage. It may be held within the three days following that event.

3. Pious and good Muslims irrespective of being rich or poor should be invited to the wedding feast. In fact, the worst wedding feast is that to which the rich are invited and the poor not.

4. The wedding feast may include one sheep or more if possible. It can also be celebrated by serving other things such as sweets and simple refreshments.

5. Invited guests and relatives who are financially able, may contribute money or food to help alleviate the cost of the feast for the husband.

6. Guests and relatives must be invited officially and by name.

7. The bride is allowed to serve the guests, as long as this is unlikely to arouse men's interest.

8. Since the wedding feast is an occasion for asking God's blessing, un-Islamic elements, such as mixing of the sexes, serving alcoholic beverages, etc. are forbidden.

Polygamy

1. It is required in Islam that when a man who already has one wife marries a virgin he should stay with her

for seven nights, and then divide the time equally between her and his first wife, but if he marries a woman who has been previously married, he should stay with her three nights and then divide his time between his wives.

2. Treating and visiting wives equally must be strictly adhered to under all circumstances.
3. If the husband becomes ill, then the question of which of his wives he will stay with is to be decided by them.
4. Making love to his wives equally is not required. What is required of the husband is to divide the time between his wives and stay a night with each of them.
5. Whenever the husband intends to travel, he must draw lots to decide which wife will accompany him.
6. The same procedure must be followed if the husband intends to perform pilgrimage or *'umrah*.
7. The husband may sleep with a wife whose day has not yet come if she has been given the day by the wife whose turn it was.
8. If a man cannot establish equality and justice among his wives, in those matters over which he has full control (i.e. excluding impulses and instincts of the heart), then he should not marry more than one wife.

13

Births

The Announcement

1. If it happens that someone is the first to know of the birth of a baby to a friend, then he should take the initiative and bring the news to him.

2. News of the birth of a girl should be welcomed exactly as news of a boy's birth and one should be grateful to God.

3. The first thing to be done for the baby is to chant the *adhān*, the call to prayer, in its ear.

4. The second thing, though not compulsory, is to chew a date until it is fine pulp and then place some of the liquid in the baby's mouth, afterwards saying a prayer for the baby. This is known as *taḥnīk* and it was sometimes done by the Prophet.

5. The necessity of naming the child as quickly as possible should be emphasized; on name-giving see Chapter 14.

6. If the child is hermaphrodite, it is given a name which can belong to a boy as well as to a girl.

7. If the child is born dead, it is nevertheless given a name.

Congratulations and Visits

1. Congratulating the parents upon the arrival of a new baby is a sign of sharing the joy of the birth with them. Congratulations can be expressed in any form, but should include wishes for blessings upon the baby, and upon the parents the blessing of being able to thank God for the birth.

2. It is completely un-Islamic conduct to express congratulations and good wishes on the birth of a boy, but to refrain from doing so on the birth of a girl.

3. The response to congratulations is to say thanks and add, 'May God show His blessing to you and grant you a child too.'

Seventh-Day Celebration

The family celebrates the birth of a new baby on the seventh day after its birth. This celebration has two major elements – slaughtering an animal and shaving the child's head.

Slaughtering an Animal

To acknowledge God's blessing and to ask Him to protect the newly-born child, the family slaughters an animal. The tradition enjoins the following rules:

1. The rightful way is to slaughter an animal on this occasion and not to give its value in alms.

2. The animal should be a sheep, goat, cow or camel, male or female.

3. The requirements in choosing the animal are the same as for the Feast of Sacrifice (see Chapter 11).

4. It is recommended that one sheep or goat be slaughtered

in the case of the birth of a girl and two sheep or goats in the case of the birth of a boy.

5. The person slaughtering the animal should say: *Bismillāh, Allāhumma, hādhā minka wa ilayka* (In the name of Allah. O God, this is done for Your sake only).

6. It is completely forbidden to splash the child's head, the walls or anything else with the animal's blood.

7. The animal's meat may preferably be divided into three lots – one to be consumed by the family, the other two may be distributed among relatives, neighbours and the poor.

8. The animal's skin, head or limbs may not be sold or given to the butcher or the cook to meet fees.

9. Some relatives and friends should be invited to dine with the family.

Shaving the Child's Head

On the seventh day after birth the child's head should be shaved. It is recommended that the hair then be weighed and the equivalent weight in silver given as alms to the poor and needy. On the same day, and after shaving, saffron, if available, may be rubbed onto the child's head.

Piercing the ears of female babies, so that they may wear ear-rings later, is allowed.

Circumcision Ceremony

1. Every Muslim boy should be circumcized. This tradition in Islam is traced back to the Prophet Ibrāhīm, peace be on him.

2. The duty of performing circumcision should be entrusted to someone well qualified to carry out this responsibility.

3. In a circumcision the foreskin must be removed in order to expose the head of the penis; it is not necessary, however, for the foreskin in its entire length and breadth to be removed.

4. If a boy is born without a foreskin, there is naturally no reason for circumcision.

5. If the child's health or condition do not permit the circumcision to be carried out, then it must be postponed to a later date.

6. It is recommended that circumcision be performed on those who embrace Islam, whether they be young or old unless it endangers their health.

7. It is preferable that circumcision is carried out as soon as possible after birth. However, the advice of a physician should be taken if it is believed that the operation should be delayed on medical grounds.

8. Godparents and other elements of 'christening' are forbidden in Islam.

14

Giving Names and Addressing Others

There is no doubt of the importance in any society of giving names. The following are some rules for giving names in the Islamic society.

Giving Names

1. Parents should not delay in giving a name to a recently-born child; they should do so as soon as possible, preferably within seven days of the birth.

2. If the parents have agreed on the choice of name, well and good. If not, then it is the right of the father to name the child.

3. It is recommended that parents give children good, beautiful and meaningful names.

    (a) Some of the best names are: 'Abdullāh, 'Abd al-Raḥmān, and Al-Ḥārith.

    (b) Names consisting of two parts, the first of which is *'Abd* (slave) compounded with one of Allah's names are considered beautiful.

    (c) Children may be given the names of Prophets.

(d) Names of angels, such as Gabriel, should be avoided.

(e) Names which declare the person as possessing excellent moral characteristics, such as purity, honesty, obedience or piousness, should be avoided.

(f) Names meaning slavery to somebody other than God (such as 'Abd al-Ḥusayn (slave of Ḥusayn) or 'Abd al-Nabī (slave of the Prophet)) are forbidden in Islam.

(g) Names indicating sadness, war and similar conditions, such as Ḥuzn, Ḥarb, etc., should be avoided.

(h) The main elements of the full name are first name, father's name, and surname. Every child must be brought into relation to his father and called by his real father's surname. That applies to the married woman who should retain her own family name and not relinquish it in favour of her husband's. That would amount to a humiliation for her and must be avoided.

(i) Having and giving good names is important not only for people, it is also required when naming streets, squares, towns, etc.

(j) Changing names of people or places when necessary should not be rejected. Changing forbidden names is considered a necessity.

Addressing Others

1. Calling out to people from a distance in the street, market or other public place is not polite conduct. It is better to approach close to the person before hailing him.

2. People can be called either by their names or their agnomens.

3. Calling a teacher or parents by their first name should be avoided, as that is a sign of impoliteness.

4. Shortening or apocopation of a name is a suitable way of calling others provided they are satisfied with it.

5. Calling another person by a certain title or agnomen must have the full approval of the person concerned.

6. If someone wants to call to a person whom he does not know, then it is best to use general terms that will not insult him, such as 'friend', 'brother'.

7. Calling a non-Muslim or corrupt individual by a patronymic (Abū so-and-so/'Umm so-and-so) is an abhorrent practice unless necessary for identification purposes.

15

Social Life

Good Social Relations

Relations between individuals in an Islamic community can be harmonious if certain rules are adhered to. These consist, firstly, of duties toward others, secondly, cultivating essential personal characteristics, and thirdly, avoiding bad personal characteristics.

Duties Toward Others

1. Speech is an important element and an important means of social relations. It is therefore essential that what is said and how it is said are wisely considered.

2. Honesty makes a person likeable and helps in building and strengthening social bonds. It is also an essential attribute of a good Muslim.

3. Amiable facial expressions during conversation are of great importance and should be understood as part of a person's duty towards others.

4. A Muslim should judge people by their deeds. He should treat well those who treat him well. No man knows another's hidden intentions and feelings – those are for God to judge. But he who shows evil, is not to be trusted, even if he expresses good intentions.

5. Relations with others should be based on respect and kindness.

6. A Muslim should make sure before making a promise that he can keep it. He should not break promises by making excuses, thinking this will be enough. To think that others' acceptance of his excuses is the end of the matter leaves a bad effect on him.

7. Care should be taken not to make many promises at one time or to many people, lest one is unable to keep them.

8. Among social duties towards others is to visit them if they become sick and to attend the funerals of their dead.

9. 'He who does not thank people does not thank God'[1] *(Ḥadīth)*. The best way for a Muslim to thank a person for doing good to him is to say: *Jazāk Allāh Khayran* (May God reward you well).

10. A Muslim should help anyone who seeks his help, unless he asks for something forbidden or undesirable. He should not hesitate to do good to others, especially when asked to do so.

11. It is a duty to accept invitations; an important one not to be turned down is to a wedding ceremony.

12. It is a Muslim's duty not to displease others with unpleasant odours from his clothes, body or mouth such as that caused by onions or garlic.

Essential Personal Characteristics

Generally speaking, there is no goodness better than a good character. The best people are those with the best character, and the worst people are those with an evil character. The following are some aspects of a positive character which should be aspired to. A Muslim should:

---

1. Abū Dā'ūd, *Ādāb*; Tirmidhī, *Birr*.

1. Be humble and should not boast to others.
2. Fulfil his trust when put in a position of trust.
3. Speak the truth always, and carry out his actions in accordance with it.
4. Show mercy and tenderness to others, Muslims and non-Muslims alike.
5. Supply help to one who needs help, and aid the distressed, even though he is not asked to do so.
6. Forgive when in a position of power and authority.
7. Harbour good thoughts of others.
8. Be disposed in friendship to others, and treat them in a friendly way.
9. Advise sincerely when consulted by others.
10. Leave alone and never speak about what does not concern him.
11. Never ask others for anything unless it is urgent or necessary.
12. Keep his appointments.
13. Restrain his anger and refrain from negative reactions.
14. Attach special importance to his relationship with those who practise Islam.
15. Be patient always.
16. Greet whom he has quarrelled with previously.
17. Guarantee the well-being of his family and kin.
18. Be modest.
19. Be satisfied and contented with what is given to him by God.
20. Put trivialities aside, concentrate on important things.

21. Be wise when dealing with evil people.
22. Exchange gifts with others.
23. Guide those towards good deeds who want to perform good deeds.
24. Mediate between disagreeing parties.
25. Contemplate his actions before performing them.
26. Be kind to others.
27. Keep secret that which others have confided to him or he has discovered about others.
28. Ask forgiveness if he has committed a deed affecting a Muslim's honour.
29. Forgive someone who has treated him badly, as though he were a close friend.
30. Meet others with a cheerful countenance.
31. Mix with others, if they are good; if not, then solitude is better for him.
32. Defend others who are absent when they are slandered in his presence.
33. Direct someone who has lost his way, especially someone who has bad eyesight.
34. Be uncomplicated but not naive.
35. Be generous, but without extravagance.
36. Show gentleness toward the weak and affection toward his parents.
37. Not take revenge on someone who reviles or reproaches him for something he knows about him, by reproaching that person for something he knows about him.

Bad Personal Characteristics

To be successful in developing social relations, it is necessary to avoid some negative characteristics and just as necessary to practise some positive ones. The following are a list of negative characteristics.

A Muslim should avoid:

1. Being nervous, highly strung or liable to sudden anger.
2. Bad relations with others.
3. Speaking about what does not concern him.
4. Arrogance, especially if it comes from a poor person, who considers himself to be great but is in fact, not so in the eyes of others.
5. Slandering anybody.
6. Listening to other people's talk when they do not want him to hear, or they are trying to avoid him.
7. Being two-faced.
8. Reviling other people's genealogies.
9. Displaying pleasure at a fellow-Muslim's misfortune.
10. Boasting about ancestors who have died or who are of high rank.
11. Seeking out others' faults in order to expose them.
12. Avoiding a Muslim for more than three days, if he has had difficulties with him.
13. Being a mischief-maker, spreading slander.
14. Saying something about a Muslim which he or she dislikes even if what he says of him or her is true.
15. Being suspicious of others.
16. Being inquisitive about others.

17. Spying.
18. Bidding against another in order to raise the price of a commodity.
19. Envying others.
20. Hating other Muslims.
21. Speaking evil of others behind their back.
22. Ridiculing others; laughing, scoffing or jeering at them.
23. Acting dishonestly toward others, deceiving and misleading them.
24. Self-deception or self-delusion.
25. Being avaricious and miserly.
26. Being a coward, unable to control his fear and running away from danger.
27. Grumbling and complaining and never being satisfied with anything.
28. Drawing attention to his own helpfulness, charity, or generosity.
29. Being selfish, thinking chiefly of and being interested in his own needs and welfare without care for others.
30. Withholding help, when he is able to offer it to others.
31. Praising and flattering somebody in his presence.
32. Showing undue respect to those of a sinful nature, or those who are wealthy or have a high position.
33. Speaking loudly.
34. Being harsh or rude to others.
35. Praising himself or over-estimating himself.
36. Lying.

Talking and Listening

Talking is an important means of communication, it is also an extension and expression of a person's personality.

1. Moderation in speech is an excellent quality, which a good Muslim should cultivate. A *Ḥadīth* says that one should either speak good or keep silent.

2. A Muslim should not talk just for the sake of talking because he thinks it is a shortcoming to be silent. The shortcoming lies in talking badly and talking too much. His duty is to say what is good or to keep silent. While being silent is a good characteristic, it should not be overdone to the extent of annoying others.

3. A Muslim should adhere to the truth and speak it whether pleased or displeased. He should speak the truth, even if it is bitter.

4. A Muslim should think carefully before speaking, and avoid saying something that he might regret and for which he would have to apologize.

5. Simplicity and clarity should characterize speech; enunciating over-carefully and speaking gutturally should be avoided. Using strange archaic words, in an attempt to demonstrate linguistic ability or to show that one is more knowledgeable than others, is forbidden.

6. Looking pleasantly at others when speaking to them is required as a courtesy.

7. There is a specific topic related to every occasion. Decorum, appropriateness, should exist between the topic discussed and the occasion.

8. A Muslim should be sure of the truthfulness and accuracy of what he says.

9. If those listening to a person cannot follow him and need to have his words repeated, it is courteous to repeat them.

10. One should not speak hurriedly. It is better to speak neither too slowly nor too quickly, neither too loudly nor too softly, for such ways of speaking tire the listener. Nor should words be interspersed with long pauses, as this will bore the listener.

Language Preferred in Speech

1. Colloquial and slang words and expressions should be avoided as much as possible.

2. Foreign words and terms should be avoided.

3. One should try to attain to a pleasant, agreeable and moral mode of expression.

4. It is not fitting for a Muslim to be given to cursing. He must never invoke God's curse, God's anger, or Hell on another.

5. A Muslim should not be given to using bad or objectionable language and should guard against speaking slander and abuse. Being of those whom others leave alone for fear of their ridicule or ribaldry casts a bad light on one's personality and character.

6. Reviling the dead is bad conduct, and is forbidden to the same degree as reviling the living.

7. Objecting to his destiny and attributing injustice to God ill-befit a Muslim and must be avoided.

8. It is a bad thing to express an over-permissive attitude toward others, especially Muslims, or to life in general.

9. Calling down evil upon himself, his children, his servants, etc. is forbidden to a Muslim.

10. Certain expressions that contradict the basic tenets of Islamic faith – for example, expressions that seem to ascribe partners to God – must be avoided. A Muslim should never say: 'What God wills and so-and-so wills';

rather he should say: 'What God alone wills' or 'What God wills and afterwards so-and-so wills.' He must never say: 'I have no supporter but God and you', but rather say: 'I have no supporter but God and afterwards you.' He should never say: 'I swear by so-and-so.'

11. To revile the wind, rain or other natural phenomena is forbidden, for these are under God's command. Instead of reviling the wind or rain, one should say: 'O God, make it a blessing and not a punishment.' Also, the rooster should not be reviled, for he wakes people for the dawn prayer.

12. A woman must not become the intimate of another woman and then describe the latter to her husband.

13. A Muslim should not try to display superior knowledge of a topic discussed; he should avoid over-use of the pronoun 'I'.

14. It is better to be gentle when blaming others for something they might have done and to avoid doing so before other people.

15. However good a Muslim may be, he should not disgrace or revile another's beliefs or character directly or indirectly.

16. A Muslim should be careful not to say anything that might give offence or be passed on, and perhaps misquoted. Subjects that might lead to embarrassment should be avoided.

17. Just as a Muslim should not disgrace or revile others in his speech, he also should not disgrace or revile himself.

18. A Muslim should never praise another in his presence. If he cannot avoid it, he should be moderate in his expression; it is for God to declare anyone pure.

19. It is a Muslim's duty to stop anyone who continually criticizes others.

20. Discussing personal and family secrets with others should be avoided; it is better to keep such things to oneself.

21. A Muslim should never allow others to tell him bad things about some third person, for it is better to meet and mix with others with no ill-feelings. If he hears people talking unjustly about others, it is his duty to defend the person spoken about.

22. After having done something a Muslim should not express the wish that he had not done it or had done it another way.

23. Speaking for too long is a bad characteristic. Being moderate when speaking is better.

24. A Muslim should avoid talking about things which do not concern him.

25. Eavesdropping on the private conversation of others should be avoided.

26. The term 'brother' should be confined to fellow Muslims.

27. Calling a Muslim an infidel or accusing him of unbelief is completely forbidden.

28. Inquiring about something from someone should be preceded by greeting the person first, taking into consideration what he is engaged in at that moment, and then confining oneself to the necessary matter.

29. It is a part of courtesy that when a Muslim mentions the Prophet or when he is mentioned in his presence he should invoke a blessing on him by saying: *Ṣallal-Lāh 'alayhi wa sallam* (Allah's blessing and peace be upon him).

30. A Muslim may not use absolute and assertive terms about future events without referring to God's will by saying: *inshā' Allāh* (If God wills).

31. A Muslim should not abuse or revile another person or speak of his faults, even if that person abuses and reviles him and even though he speaks of his faults.

Listening

A Muslim should:

1. Try to listen to others as politely as possible.
2. Avoid interrupting others when they are speaking.
3. Face the person he is speaking to and show interest in what he is saying, even if he is not interested in the topic being discussed, try to control himself, unless the topic is directed against Islam, its principles or the Prophet, in which case he should either try to put an end to it or leave.
4. Avoid getting involved in a pointless argument with someone who expresses views with which he does not agree.

Swearing

1. As far as possible, swearing and taking an oath should be avoided.
2. A Muslim should swear by Allah, one of His attributes or names, only. He is not allowed to swear by something else, such as the Prophet, Prayer, the Ka'bah, the Qur'ān, etc.
3. Swearing in Allah's name, unfaithfully, is considered a great sin.
4. Using the colloquial expression 'by God' should be avoided.
5. If a Muslim swears to do something or to refrain from doing something, and afterwards he finds doing some-

thing else is better, he is recommended not to carry out his oath and to make proper atonement.

6. It is a Muslim's duty to fulfil his oath. Therefore, he must be sure before swearing that he has the means to carry out his promise.

7. Using the threat: 'If you don't do this or that, I will divorce my wife', is distasteful and unbecoming to a Muslim. Marriage must not be referred to in such a trivial and childish manner.

8. Swearing oaths should be avoided in certain cases, for example, in business or financial transactions.

9. Breaking an oath must be avoided. If a Muslim breaks his oath then he must make atonement by providing food for a meal for ten poor people or providing each of the ten with one article of clothing. If he is not financially able to do this, then he must fast three successive days.

10. If a Muslim vows to do something forbidden in Islam, such as to take something which does not belong to him, then it is his duty to break his oath.

11. If a Muslim vows to do something not recommended by Islam, then he is advised not to fulfil his oath and to make atonement.

Nadhr (to connect a vow with the fulfilment of a wish)

1. To vow, in return for a favour from God to oneself, to do some specific thing for the sake of God, is permitted but is not recommended.

2. Vowing to oneself to do a certain thing should be done only for the sake of God.

3. A Muslim must fulfil his vow pledged for the sake of God, and may avoid fulfilling it if pledged for the sake of someone else.

4. It is not permissible for someone who has made a vow to slaughter an animal for the sake of Allah, to eat anything of it unless his initial intention included the stipulation that he would eat some.

Laughter

1. There are many reasons for laughing, such as seeing a pleasant thing, hearing good news or a joke.
2. To laugh because other people laugh is not recommended; there should be a reason for laughter.
3. Laughter should not be characterized by loud or unpleasant sounds.
4. A broad smile, such as makes the back teeth visible, is better than laughing.
5. It is better always to control the sounds of laughter; excessive noise should be avoided.
6. It is not fitting for a Muslim to make people laugh for the sake of laughter, especially if that leads to lying.
7. One should not sit with people amongst whom is a person trying to make them laugh at any expense.
8. Laughing in ridicule of another person must be avoided.

Weeping

1. Weeping should be spontaneous and for a good reason.
2. It is not unmanly to cry because emotions should not be suppressed. Yet it should be done with restraint and not with excessive or loud sounds.

Jokes

1. It is good to share jokes with others, because always being serious is burdensome.

2. When making jokes, it is better to avoid using impolite or hurtful terms, directly or indirectly.

3. Over-seriousness and excessive joking should both be avoided because they will lessen self-esteem and risk hurting others' feelings.

4. Attention should be given to the context in which the joke is told so as to avoid hurting others' feelings.

5. A joke should not be accompanied with excessive gestures or bodily movements.

6. One should not take what belongs to others while joking.

7. To terrify others, in jest, is forbidden.

8. Lying is not allowed even for joking purposes.

Behaviour When Meeting Others

A Muslim should observe the following:

1. He should smile, for a smile is the key to a successful meeting. However, he should not smile at people because of their material wealth.

2. He should be first to salute other Muslims.

3. He should not bow to any person when saluting, no matter who he is and whatever the occasion.

4. When meeting others and after saluting, he should extend his right hand and shake hands; this enhances mutual respect.

5. He should not shake hands with anyone for whom it might be a nuisance.

6. If his hand is dirty and someone wants to shake hands with him, he should politely excuse himself, explaining the reason.

7. He should not feel upset about shaking hands at every meeting.

8. Men shake hands with men, women with women. If a woman wants to shake hands with a man or vice versa, he/she should excuse himself/herself.

9. Too many questions about the family, etc. when meeting is a time-wasting activity and is likely to lead to boredom, so he should avoid it.

10. If anyone meets him and begins a conversation before saluting him, he has the right not to speak to him.

11. If he is seated, it is not necessary for him to stand up to shake hands. Although there are certain occasions when he may stand up, such as meeting someone who has returned from a journey.

12. There is no objection to him kissing the hand of a Muslim scholar or of his parents. However, this gesture is forbidden in the case of a wealthy or powerful person. In the first case it is allowed on condition that kissing the hand does not replace shaking hands.

13. When a meeting is finished he should extend his hand to shake hands once again, saying: *Assalāmu ‘alaykum* (Peace be upon you).

14. He should not shake hands with someone who has a contagious disease.

15. It is not *sunnah* for him to shake hands after praying, saying: *Taqabbal Allāh* (May God accept our prayer).

Manners of Greeting

1. The habit of greeting is of great importance for it increases friendship and acquaintance. It is also an act of kindness and courtesy.

2. A person who is riding should greet one who is walking, a person who is walking should greet one who is sitting, and a small group should greet a larger one. The young should greet the old. If two people of more or less the same age and both walking meet each other, either may greet the other first.

3. Flexibility should characterize observance of the above-mentioned rules, for the best of people are those who do not hesitate to greet others.

4. Others should be greeted by saying: *Assalāmu 'alaykum* (Peace be upon you).

5. Using other expressions of greeting, such as 'good morning', 'good evening', 'hello', are allowed only after saying: *Assalāmu 'alaykum*.

6. Politeness requires that a salutation be returned in the same or better way. Required, at least, is that one says: *Wa 'alaykum assalām* (Upon you be peace) and the ideal and perfect form is: *Wa 'alaykum assalām wa raḥmatu Allah wa barakātuh* (Upon you be peace, God's mercy and His blessings).

7. It is a Muslim's duty to respond to a salutation by returning it without delay, unless there is a good reason for delay.

8. When a Muslim greets others or is greeted by others, his greeting or response to the other's greeting should be done audibly.

9. If a Muslim thinks that the other did not hear his greeting for some reason, then it is his duty to greet him another time, even for a third time, but not more.

10. If meeting others is repeated within a certain period of time, it should not be thought boring or monotonous to greet them again.

11. Greeting others by making a gesture with the fingers, with the palm of the hand, or with the head must be avoided.

12. A Muslim should greet both those whom he knows and those whom he does not know. This increases the number of his acquaintances and friends. He cannot, however, in certain cases, such as at markets or on crowded streets, give salutations to everyone he passes or meets.

13. If passing a company of people, a Muslim should not greet some of them by mentioning their names or titles. Politeness requires him to greet them all in general terms, so that everyone is greeted.

14. When greeted by a company of people the salutation should be returned with a general greeting and without specifying anyone in particular.

15. If someone passes a Muslim, and he is in doubt of his greeting, he is not required to respond to him.

16. If someone greets a company of people, and his greeting is returned by a member of this company then this is enough, though it is recommended that all members respond.

17. It is a Muslim's duty to respond to another's greeting whether he is a Muslim or non-Muslim.

18. If a Muslim meets someone and he is in doubt whether he will return his greeting, it is nonetheless his duty to greet him.

19. Though greeting others is recommended there are certain cases where salutations should be avoided, such

as greeting someone who is in the act of relieving himself, or sleeping, or drowsing.

20. If a Muslim passes a mixed company of Muslims and non-Muslims, he should greet them by saying: *Assalāmu 'alaykum* (Peace be upon you).

21. If a Muslim is greeted while relieving himself, he should not respond until he leaves the lavatory.

22. A Muslim should not neglect to greet members of his family upon returning home.

23. If passing children, it is better to greet them, even though they are supposed to greet one first.

24. If someone has sent another person to a Muslim with a message which includes a greeting, he must greet both of them by saying: *Assalāmu 'alayka wa 'alaiyhi* (Peace be upon you and upon him).

25. If sending a message to a non-Muslim, he may be greeted by writing: *Assalāmu 'alā man ittaba'a al-hudā* (Peace be upon who follows the right path).

26. When approaching a group of people or meeting a person, a salutation should be given. When parting, a salutation should again be given at the end of the meeting. It is of particular importance to greet when parting; especially in the case of two parties who may have argued or disagreed during their conversation, for the greeting implies that there are no hard feelings and that both attach value to a continuing good relationship.

27. When greeting other Muslims, whether orally (on the telephone) or by writing (letters, etc.), one should start and finish with: *Assalāmu 'alaykum.*

28. It is not un-Islamic to greet non-Muslims, but a Muslim should not use: *Assalāmu 'alaykum.*

Asking Permission to Enter Another's House

1. A Muslim may not enter another's house before asking permission to do so. Politeness requires such permission, even from those who are very close to him, such as his parents, for people in their homes may be in a state of dress or of mood in which they do not wish to be seen. This is especially important in regard to women who must have time to arrange themselves, to cover their hair, and so on.

2. It is forbidden to glance into someone else's house when the door is opened to greet one.

3. The visitor must greet whoever answers the door before asking permission to enter. The manner of asking permission to enter should be thus: *'Assalāmu 'alaykum*, may I enter?', or *'Assalāmu 'alaykum*, may (mention your name) enter?' Refusal of permission to enter is justified in the absence of a greeting first.

4. If the visitor is asked to give his identity before the door is opened to him, he must give it. To say merely: 'It is me', is insufficient and not approved.

5. The request to enter, if permission is not granted, may be repeated three times. If permission is still not granted, the visitor should leave. If the caller does not have an appointment, then the person he wants to visit is not required to receive him. Therefore, he should not take offence if he informs him that he is busy and would rather not receive guests at this time.

6. Knocking at the door or ringing the bell is not a substitute for giving a greeting and asking permission to enter.

7. Knocking at the door should be done gently, for there might be someone asleep or ill inside the house. If after knocking at the door three times there is no response, the caller should leave.

At a Friend's House

Exchange of visits strengthens relationships between individuals and is valued as one of the main elements in a healthy social life. It eradicates that social isolation which is not acceptable within Islam.

1. It is a recommended Islamic procedure that a Muslim should inform his host of his intention to visit him. If he visits somebody without a previous appointment, and he is unwilling to receive him for one reason or another, he should not be upset.

2. Appointments must be kept promptly. If there is just cause for changing or cancelling the appointment then either party should properly inform the other.

3. Suitable times to pay a visit do not include night time, evening (after *'Ishā'* prayer) or the siesta hour.

4. It is the duty of the host to receive the guest if there is an appointment. Otherwise, the host has the right to apologize for not being able to receive him. In this case the guest should not feel offended.

5. Visits should be free of any personal interest or other selfishness. The aim of visiting should be to strengthen brotherly relations with other Muslims, for the sake of God.

6. Men should not visit women whose husbands are away from home, unless they are *maḥrams* to the women visited.

7. A Muslim may not enter the host's house until he has his permission, and has greeted him, even if he has an appointment with him.

8. A visitor should remember that he is in someone else's home. Therefore, he should try his best to fit in with the plans made by his host, even if he finds things a little boring.

9. A Muslim should not limit his visits only to those who visit him.

10. A guest must not lead a host in prayer or sit in the host's accustomed place without his permission.

11. Social intercourse and mixing between men and women when visiting other families is forbidden. A guest is allowed to speak to the wife or daughters of the host if there is a need. The host's wife can serve the guests provided she dresses and behaves correctly.

12. A woman may not visit others if her husband objects.

13. Open violation of Islamic teachings by the host or members of his family should cause the guest to leave. Such behaviour is unacceptable and intolerable to good Muslims. The host in this case is requested to show understanding toward the guest's behaviour.

14. If a Muslim wants to stay as a guest with someone then he should not expect his hospitality to continue for more than three days. Anything beyond that, he receives as charity. A guest should not stay so long as to make himself an encumbrance.

15. It is impolite for a guest to refuse what a host offers him unless there is a medical reason or he is fasting. In this case he must apologize and explain the reason to him.

16. If a visitor wants to relieve himself he should first inform the host. He should not leave his place until permission is given.

17. When visiting others, it is not proper to stay long unless requested to do so. Becoming a nuisance by remaining too long and overstaying as a guest is not proper Islamic conduct.

18. When the time comes to leave, a visitor should thank the host for his entertainment. He should ask permission

to leave, and not move until permission is given. He should bid the host farewell.

19. If a Muslim intends to fast while staying with others as a guest, then it is polite to inform the host of his intention.

20. If a friend or relative does not visit him, a Muslim should not accord him the same treatment. He should call on him and not wait for him to return his visit.

21. A Muslim should not limit his visits to only special occasions. As mentioned above, exchange of visits between individuals is always beneficial.

Receiving Guests

1. A Muslim host should receive his guests heartily and with a welcoming smile. To honour and entertain a guest is an Islamic duty.

2. It is the host's duty to keep all sources of annoyance away from his guests.

3. It is impolite to ask the guest to perform any service.

4. The guest needs no invitation to come and stay for a number of days, though it is better if the visitor can inform the host in advance of his arrival. The guest can stay three days and then should leave.

5. If a guest comes to visit a Muslim, it is his duty, if he is able, to be hospitable and generous by offering him food and drink, whether or not he receives the same treatment when he visits him.

6. When the visit is ended and the guest is about to leave, the host should accompany him to the outside door and give him a good farewell.

Inviting Others to Dine

1. Inviting others to dine is recommended, provided a Muslim's intention is not to boast about his own achievements.

2. Invitations to a banquet should not be confined to the rich and influential, the poor and needy should be included too.

3. Invitations to dine should be restricted to good Muslims, though inviting others is not forbidden. Priority should be given to Muslims, however, since a result of dining together is a strengthening of friendship and brotherhood and this aim should be reserved for fellow Muslims.

4. It is recommended that neighbours are among those invited to dine.

5. Showing generosity to invited guests is an important matter, provided exaggeration and extravagance are avoided.

6. The manners of receiving a guest, discussed in Chapter 15, should be adhered to.

7. Although the guests may begin eating as soon as the meal is served, it is nevertheless good conduct to indicate to the guests that they should begin by saying: *Bismillāh* (In the name of God).

8. It is polite and considered a form of generosity to urge guests to eat and drink, but not to excess, and not to insist that they eat a certain kind of food.

9. A Muslim should be careful when speaking not to praise his own generosity or his own table.

10. Restricting invitations to dine only to special occasions is not recommended; an invitation may be offered at any time.

11. A host should avoid giving his guests the impression that he is observing how much he eats or that he thinks he is eating too much.

12. If a guest arrives unexpectedly, it is a Muslim's duty to see that he is adequately cared for.

When Invited to a Meal

1. If a Muslim is invited to a meal, it is recommended that he accepts. It is obligatory to accept a wedding feast invitation (though not if it entails forbidden things).

2. An invitation to a meal from anybody who is extending the invitation only out of personal interest should be declined.

3. If a Muslim is invited by someone to a meal while fasting voluntarily, then he is free either to break his fast or to visit him and keep his fast.

4. When going to a meal in somebody's house, a Muslim should not take anyone with him who has not been invited.

5. If someone follows a Muslim and accompanies him without his consent when he is going to his hosts, it is his duty to inform the host of the situation. The host may accept or reject the uninvited guest, as he wishes.

6. When the meal is served, it is not good manners to rush to the table. It is correct to follow the person who is to one's right.

7. The invitations of people competing with each other to provide a feast for the sake of ostentation, should not be accepted.

8. An invitation from a morally corrupt person should not be accepted merely because one does not wish to say

no to him. The invitation may be accepted only if the intention is to bring him back to Islam, otherwise not.

9. When sitting down to eat, proper table manners should be observed, as discussed in Chapter 4.

10. If something among the dishes or drink offered to a Muslim is forbidden according to Islam, such as wine or pork, then he should inform the host of the necessity of removing it, otherwise of his leaving, and if it is not removed he should leave immediately.

11. A guest should thank the host for his invitation and ask God to bless him. The following *du'ā'* may be recited: *Akala ṭa'āmukum al-abrār, wa ṣalla 'alaykum al-Malā'ika wa afṭara 'indakum aṣ-Ṣā'imūn* (May the righteous eat your food, may the angels invoke blessings on you, and may those who have been fasting break their fast with you).

Visiting the Sick

1. Visiting the sick is one way of expressing concern for them, and it helps them feel better. It also strengthens and develops social relations. So, the sick should be visited, not only among friends and relatives, but also those who are not immediate relations or acquaintances.

2. Making an appointment to visit the sick is a good thing but not necessary. One should keep in mind the proper visiting times if the sick are in hospital, and comply with all regulations, including those prohibiting taking food and drinks.

3. The kind of sickness determines the nature and length of the visit. Visitors may be prevented by doctors from seeing the sick person or they may be allowed a brief visit. If doctors permit, it is recommended to stay long enough for the sick person to feel that he/she is not neglected.

4. A visitor should sit close to the sick person and ask how he/she feels.

5. When visiting a patient one is recommended to pray for his/her recovery and that the sickness may be the cause of purification of sins. The Prophet used to say to the patients he visited: *Lā ba's Ṭahūr inshā'Allāh* (No harm will come; it is a purification, if God wills).

6. A visitor should select his consoling words with care; avoiding any mention of objection to destiny, describing the sickness as evil, or any words that might have a bad effect on the sick person. Instead, he/she should be encouraged to accept the illness as something that God has planned and that one must think well of God.

7. If the sick person has reached a hopeless state a Muslim may say: *Innā li-llāh wa-innā ilayhi rāji'ūn* (We belong to God and to Him we return).

8. A Muslim should not deprive the sick person of his visits; he should make them as frequently as necessary, especially if the sick person feels close to him.

9. Concern for the patient should not be limited to visiting him; one is also required to ask his family, from time to time, about his health.

10. It is permissible to visit a non-Muslim who is sick if he happens to be a friend, neighbour or relative, or if one seeks to persuade him to become a Muslim.

11. To stare at a leperous person or at others with similar diseases or deformities, should be avoided lest they feel looked down upon.

Group Meetings

1. Socializing, just to kill time, should be avoided. Time is a precious asset not to be wasted. Rather, it should

be spent on useful affairs. Also, friends should be selected carefully.

2. Places for a gathering should be respectable, such as private houses and mosques, not pavements, markets, etc.

3. Socializing, if one's body, clothes or mouth smell bad, should be avoided.

4. After seeking permission to enter and greeting the house owner, a Muslim should next greet the people seated. He should shake hands with everyone, starting from the right and sit where he finds himself when he has finished.

5. When joining a gathering, a person should sit where a place is made for him; otherwise he should sit in any vacant place.

6. If someone offers his place to someone joining the gathering, he should apologize politely for not accepting it and sit where he finds himself or where someone makes room without getting up, or where there is enough room.

7. One should be careful not to oblige anyone to leave his seat, even a child, in order to take his place.

8. It is not fitting to sit between two people unless permission is given, because they may be talking privately or expressing some intimacy.

9. Care must be taken when sitting not to turn one's back on anyone, since this might be interpreted as a form of dislike or disrespect.

10. If more people join the gathering, those already seated should make room for the newcomers.

11. Someone joining a gathering should remember that those present do not have to stand up for him.

12. If someone has left his seat intending to return, he has more right to his seat and others should be careful not to take his place.

13. If the company consists of three people, any two of them must not talk privately in front of the third.

14. If two people are talking privately when a newcomer arrives, he should not obtrude uninvited upon their conversation.

15. If more than three people are present, then two of them may talk privately or intimately.

16. It is polite to listen to others and not interrupt or let one's attention wander.

17. A person's sitting posture should be humble and respectful of others.

18. It is necessary that in any gathering people should remember God and invoke blessings on His Messenger Muhammad, peace be upon him.

19. If a Muslim hears people talking about someone behind his back, he should politely try to stop them; if they persist he should excuse himself and leave.

20. What is said or done in a sitting place should continuously be noted and judged in terms of the permissible and the forbidden.

21. Any secrets that people exchange and divulge in private conversation are in confidence and should always be respected.

22. Gatherings are not recommended after *'Ishā'* prayer unless necessitated for study purposes or for the sake of a guest.

23. Those who sit in an assembly, gathering, meeting, etc., where there is much clamour or meaningless talk, are recommended, at the end of the gathering and before

getting up to leave, to say the following *du'ā'*: *Subḥānaka Allahumma wa biḥamdika ashhadu an lā ilāha illā anta astaghfiruka wa atūbu ilayka* (O Allah, I witness Your absolute transcendence, and praise You. I testify that there is no god except You; I ask Your pardon and turn to You in repentance).

Forms of Sitting

1. Sitting should be respectful of others. Stretching legs out in front of others or sitting higher up than others should be avoided.

2. Private parts should always be concealed in any sitting posture.

3. Sitting with the left hand behind the back, while leaning on the other hand, should be avoided.

4. A person should not sit with one part of his body in the sun and the other part in the shade.

5. Sitting on the floor is the best posture for eating.

Women's Conduct Outside the Home

1. A woman who has used incense, make-up, or has perfumed herself, should not leave her home until the make-up is removed and no scent of the perfume remains.

2. A man may not spend the night in the house of a woman unless he is her husband or a *maḥram*.

3. A man and a woman are not permitted to be alone together unless the man is a *maḥram* to the woman or, of course, her husband.

4. If a man should happen to look at a woman, he must turn his eyes away. An accidental glance is allowed, a second look is forbidden.

5. Social intercourse or mixing of men and women is of two kinds:

    (a) That which is related to general public life and not confined to certain groups of people, but common to all people, such as in streets, markets and mosques. Mixing in this case is allowed, provided all the above-mentioned conditions are fulfilled.

    (b) Free mixing of men and women in places confined to particular groups of people, such as in school, university or work place, is forbidden, and separation of the sexes is required.

6. Outside the home when a woman speaks to a man her speech should not be inviting, but should remain objective and crisp.

7. Women are allowed to indulge in all business transactions allowed to men; a woman may also hold a job if it does not affect her main responsibility of the house and family, if her husband agrees, and if she is not required to mix with men. For instance, a woman may teach in a girls' school or be a women's doctor.

8. When leaving work for home, a woman should remember to wear Islamic dress, as mentioned in Chapter 5.

9. Islam does not consider the house to be a woman's jail; she is allowed to leave the house, as long as there is a good reason for doing so.

Celebrations

1. The most important rules governing celebrations are:

    (a) Mixing of men and women should be avoided.

    (b) Extravagant parties and wastefulness must be avoided even if a Muslim is financially able.

2. Celebrating occasions foreign to Islam, such as Christmas, New Year, Mother's Day, Father's Day, Labour Day, wedding anniversaries, birthdays and the like, is an imitation of other cultures.

3. Certain other celebrations have also been introduced into Islam from outside – such as the Prophet's birthday, the Prophet's *Isrā'* and *Mi'rāj* (the Prophet's night journey from Makkah to Jerusalem and then to the seven heavens), the Prophet's emigration, etc.

4. Instead of forbidden occasions, Muslims are encouraged to have meetings of individual villages, towns, or city districts, to discuss different economic, political and social issues relating to the present and future; or to discuss specifically devotional matters or to read the Qur'ān and praise God.

Behaviour Toward Relatives

1. Visiting relatives and being concerned about them is extremely important.

2. There is no prescribed number of visits to relatives, but they should be frequent enough so that they do not feel neglected.

3. Whenever he meets his relatives, a Muslim should ask and concern himself about their welfare.

4. A Muslim should remember that he has a responsibility toward his poor and needy relatives. He should extend help to them and from time to time give them as a present some of the things they need.

5. If a Muslim is breast-fed by a woman other than his mother, he should remember that he has another family and relatives in breast feeding.

6. It is best not to wait for a visit from relatives before visiting them.

7. It is not good to answer an offence from a relative with the same. It shows moral stature to refrain from answering in that way.

8. A Muslim should treat his mother's sister as he treats his mother.

9. A Muslim should treat his uncle as he treats his father.

10. It is permitted for a woman to sit with male relatives (other than those she is forbidden to marry), provided:

    (a) That they act within the limits of proper decorum;

    (b) That she is not alone with one relative.

Behaviour Toward Neighbours

1. The first rule governing behaviour toward neighbours is to avoid causing them any form of material or moral harm such as by raising one's voice or having loud, noisy celebrations, especially at night.

2. Visiting neighbours is important for it helps establish amiable relations, especially on major occasions such as births, weddings, sickness and death, etc.

3. Being generous to neighbours is in accordance with the Prophet's teachings. One should invite a neighbour to dine from time to time, and send him food at other times.

4. Doing any ill to a neighbour's children should be avoided. Care should be taken not to let children's conflicts engender misunderstandings between their parents.

5. A neighbour and his family have certain special privileges on a Muslim. Extending help to them when it is needed is Islamic behaviour.

6. If a Muslim knows his neighbour to be in some financial

difficulty, he should not wait for him to ask for help, rather he should offer help if he can.

7. A Muslim should keep secrets confided in him by neighbours, or which he may have overheard.

8. A Muslim should talk well of his neighbours, defend them if people talk ill of them, because his relations with them deserve his special attention and care.

9. It is the housewife's responsibility to look after relations with women neighbours.

10. If a neighbour is a relative, good mutual relations become all the more important.

11. Good relations should not be confined to next-door neighbours but should also extend to those further away.

Gifts

Exchanging gifts between individuals is recommended by Islam, for it strengthens relations. Therefore, if a Muslim is financially able, he should try to present gifts to relatives and friends while observing the following rules:

1. Giving presents to relatives has priority over giving presents to others.

2. Spending a lot of money on extravagant gifts and a lot of time choosing them are bad habits that limit the exchange of gifts and might even lead to non-exchange of gifts.

3. A gift should only be bought with money earned in a legal way.

4. The purpose of giving others gifts must be to honour them and to strengthen relations. Giving gifts in the hope of material gain or personal influence, is bribery, which is strictly forbidden.

5. On presenting a gift, discussing anything that might

make the recipient sceptical about its purpose should be avoided.

6. On receiving a gift, a Muslim should open it and look at it, show satisfaction, and express thanks for it. If the one who sent him the gift is present, then he should pray for him.

7. Giving someone a present and then asking for it back is not polite nor, with the exception of gifts presented to children by their parents or their grandparents, is it permitted.

8. It is an act of politeness to return the courtesy of a gift received by seeking an occasion to do so.

9. A Muslim should not accept a gift from someone who intends to exploit him or profit from his authority or influence in any way. In fact, such a gift is in reality a bribe.

10. A Muslim must not accept gifts of things forbidden to be owned by him, such as a bottle of wine or pork meat.

11. If refusing a gift for one of the above reasons, one should try to explain the reason. In this case, the one who is offering the gift should not feel offended.

12. When a parent gives presents to his children he should not favour one above another.

13. It is most important to remember that giving presents is recommended, not obligatory. It is an error to believe that giving presents is required: such an error may hinder exchange of visits between people who, especially if they are not financially able, will seek to avoid such visits in order to avoid giving presents.

16

Behaviour in Various Situations

In the Mosque

1. A Muslim should put on his finest and cleanest clothes when going to the mosque, use perfume if available, and be sure that his shoes are clean.

2. A Muslim should refrain from going to the mosque if he has eaten onions or garlic, unless he is completely sure that he is free of odour, as such odour will disturb others.

3. It is best to enter the mosque and join the worshippers calmly and quietly without hurrying.

4. Pushing and shoving when entering or leaving the mosque should be avoided; those on the right should enter or leave first.

5. When entering the mosque, a Muslim should proceed with his right foot, saying: *Bismillāh, Allāhumma iftaḥ lī abwāba raḥmatik* (O Allah, open to me the gates of Your mercy).

6. A Muslim entering the mosque should, if possible, pray two *rak'ahs* before sitting down.

7. Speaking in the mosque is permitted provided the following rules are adhered to:

   (a) Using raised voices in the mosque is not right conduct.

   (b) Those who recite the Qur'ān in the mosque, should do so quietly, otherwise they will confuse or disturb those praying or reading the Qur'ān.

   (c) The mosque is not the place for selling, buying or discussing other worldly affairs. Therefore, if anyone is heard discussing buying or selling in a mosque he must be advised not to do so.

   (d) One should not sit beside people who talk about worldly affairs in the mosque.

8. Before beginning the congregational prayer, the worshippers should stand in straight lines, first men, then children, and then women. All should ensure that the lines are straight, and should stand close together and erect.

9. Entering and passing through the mosque is not unlawful for a menstruating woman or one who is seminally defiled. However, they are forbidden to remain in the mosque.

10. Mosques are the best places in this world. Therefore, Muslims should frequent them. It is a clear indication that a person is a good Muslim if he goes regularly to the mosque.

11. To pass immediately in front of a man who is saying his prayer should be avoided, for it would interfere with his prayer to do so.

12. One should not be in a hurry to leave the mosque, and when leaving should depart from the mosque with the left foot, saying: *Allāhumma innī as'aluka min faḍlika* (O Allah, I seek Your favour).

13. The movements of those praying in congregation should not precede but should follow those of the *imām*.

14. It is not recommended that a Muslim performs his prayers in the one, same spot in the mosque.

15. Using a mosque as a thoroughfare is a detestable act.

At the Cemetery

1. There are two main purposes for a Muslim to visit a cemetery: to pray for the dead, and to remind himself of the Hereafter.

2. Visiting graves is recommended. Women are permitted to visit graves, though it is recommended that they do not do so too often.

3. On visiting graves a Muslim should say: *Assalāmu 'alā ahlil diyāri minal-m'uminna wal muslimīn wa yarḥamu Allāh al-mustaqdimīna minnā wal musta'khirīn wa innā inshā'Allāhu bikum La lāhiqūn* (Peace be upon the Muslim and faithful inhabitants of the abodes. May God show mercy to those of us who go before and those who go after and God willing, we will meet you).

4. Violating Islamic teachings while at the cemetery is forbidden.

5. Nothing is to be said over the grave other than what is mentioned in (3) above, except to pray for the dead.

6. It is forbidden to touch any grave with the intention of gaining a blessing from it.

7. Putting wreaths on graves is an imitation of alien cultures.

8. Lighting candles or placing lanterns on the grave is an innovation.

9. Women, when visiting the cemetery, are requested to

avoid all kinds of behaviour violating Islam, such as wearing un-Islamic dress, wailing, etc.

10. The cemetery is not a place where people gather for collective worship at certain times of the year; visiting graves must be an occasion only to be reminded of death, which will have a positive effect on the individual's daily life and behaviour. Using the cemetery as a place of worship or celebration is utterly forbidden in Islam.

11. Sitting on the grave is forbidden.

12. There is no definite day or time for visiting the cemetery.

On the Street

Roads, streets and lanes are public property. The rules of behaviour in these places are of great importance. Observing these rules indicates civilization and progress, violating them indicates backwardness.

1. The main principle which should govern the behaviour of the individual on the road is to avoid harming or disturbing others.

2. Keeping roads tidy and clean is the responsibility of every member of the society.

3. The road is not a place for sitting or meeting, so using it in this way should be avoided.

4. Violating the rules of Islam on the roads and streets of an Islamic country is a grave matter which has repercussions for the community. So it is a Muslim's duty, if he sees something objectionable to disapprove it and to recommend what is reputable, provided that he does so in conformity with Islamic teachings and expresses himself with wisdom, restraint and good manners.

5. Guiding those who are lost and seeking direction,

helping the old or the invalid, is an Islamic duty and reflects good manners.

6. Removing anything which could be injurious or offensive or which causes annoyance to people on their way, is an Islamic duty.

7. Thinking ill of others one sees or meets on the road is un-Islamic conduct. A Muslim should think well of others.

8. Returning greetings on the road is one of the rules of courtesy.

9. Men and women should avoid mingling along the road. Women should walk on the side farthest from the road or street.

10. To stare at a woman on the road after the first glance is forbidden. So a man should lower his gaze or turn it aside.

11. To offer a lift to those who do not have their own vehicles is recommended.

12. Among rules for the use of public transport is the requirement that women and the elderly be properly respected.

13. When using public transport, a Muslim should confine himself to speaking only when necessary and then in a subdued voice, refrain from smoking, or otherwise being a nuisance to fellow travellers.

14. Crowding and rushing onto public vehicles is not civilized conduct. The principle of favouring the right when entering and leaving the vehicle should be observed.

15. Shouting when approaching someone on the road from behind is bad behaviour. It is better to come nearer to him before speaking.

16. Eating while walking along the road or street is considered un-Islamic behaviour.

17. A Muslim's manner of walking along the road is a part of his Islamic personality; it expresses to others and conveys to himself certain sentiments and attitudes. Walking, therefore, should conform to certain guidelines:

    (a) Reeling or swaying when walking are to be avoided; so too walking with an effeminate gait, or with a stance of pride, prancing or strutting; also cowering when walking.

    (b) When walking in company, one should consider others and not proceed at a pace too fast for them.

17

Funerals

Things That Need to be Done When Someone Dies

1. Notification of a person's death to friends and the public may well be through an announcement in the local press, provided that such an announcement does not praise or commend the dead person or demonstrate his esteem. Instead, the announcement would do better to ask others to pray for the dead person.

2. Preparing the corpse for burial by washing and shrouding it is necessary. This should be carried out in an inexpensive way.

3. Dead men are washed by men, dead women by women, except in the case of a married couple, where the survivor is allowed to wash the dead person.

4. The dead person should be washed with water and, if available, lotus leaves, an odd number of times, three or five, or more if necessary, beginning with the right side and, for the last washing, camphor should be added to the solution. If the dead person is a woman, then her hair should be braided into three plaits and placed behind her back.

5. Though shrouding the dead should be done with cloth of moderate quality, extravagance is not recommended

and using a coffin[1] is not allowed unless necessary for health reasons.

6. The *Shuhadā'* martyrs should be stripped of their jewellery and buried in their clothing without having the blood washed off.

7. A Muslim who dies while performing pilgrimage or *'umrah* should be washed with water and lotus leaves, if available, and shrouded in the same two pieces of cloth with which he covered himself for the pilgrimage or *'umrah*. No perfume, in this case, should be put on the dead, neither should his head be covered.[2]

8. Anyone who has washed a dead body is recommended to bathe himself and anyone who has carried it is recommended to perform ablution.

9. It is the duty of those who wash the dead not to mention to others whatever they may have noticed of the bodily imperfections of the dead person. Mentioning good things is allowed.

10. It is recommended that, immediately after washing and shrouding it, the body not be kept long, but rather taken quickly, prayed over, and then buried.

Escorting the Funeral

1. The funeral of a Muslim must be attended by other Muslims. Therefore, a Muslim should not be slow to participate in escorting the funeral, whether or not the dead person or his relatives are known to him directly.

2. Escorting a funeral consists of two stages; the first lasts till the funeral prayer is offered, and the second till the dead person is buried. It is recommended, however,

---

1. By 'coffin' here we do not mean the Arabic but the English sense of the term, i.e. a box or case in which the dead body is laid before interment.
2. The Mālikī and Hanafī schools do not support the special privilege of *kafn*, shroud for one who dies in *ihrām*.

that those attending the first stage also wait until the second stage is completed.

3. Prayer should be performed over every Muslim who dies, including infants. Taking the dead body into the mosque for the funeral prayers is not recommended. Prayers should be conducted in a place outside the mosque, e.g. in the courtyard.

4. It is not proper that some people, especially relatives of the dead, do not take part in the funeral prayers, instead waiting on others to do so in their place.

5. The pace of the procession should be neither too quick nor too slow.

6. Those following and escorting a funeral on foot should walk either in front of or behind the bier, or on the right or left, keeping near it. Those riding, however, should keep behind.

7. Following the funeral with incense or candles, mentioning God's name audibly or loudly, weeping aloud, or reading the Qur'ān aloud, are forbidden when escorting a funeral.

8. Speech should be kept short and light during the funeral procession.

9. When a Muslim sees a funeral passing he may stand up.

10. Conveying the deceased by car or other vehicle is not recommended, unless the cemetery is far away.

11. It is recommended that those who carry a bier perform ablution afterwards. This will help to refresh and reorientate them physically and emotionally.

12. Walking when following the funeral is better than riding, unless the cemetery is far away. However, on returning from the burial it is permissible to ride or walk.

Burial

1. It is a matter of great importance that a special cemetery be devoted exclusively for the use of Muslims. Muslims may not be buried in the cemeteries of non-Muslims, nor vice versa.

2. No person may be cremated, even if the dead person has specifically requested it. Such a request must not be fulfilled.

3. The dead should be interred in the cemetery, except the *Shuhadā'* (those killed on the battlefield) who should be buried where they are martyred.

4. The dead person should be buried in the locality where he died. It is undesirable that the body be taken back to the person's own country or moved to another city.

5. The burial must take place as soon as possible after death, with the following exceptions:

    (a) At night.

    (b) From sunrise until the sun is about 4.5 degrees above the horizon (when it is fully risen).

    (c) At the zenith of the sun (when it is at the meridian) until it passes the meridian.

    (d) When the sun pales before sunset until it has set.

    Burying the dead during these times is forbidden unless there is an urgent necessity.

6. Allocating a special cemetery for state leaders or for the rich is utterly forbidden. Islam rejects the class system in life and at death.

7. When more than one person is to be buried in a single grave, e.g. in the case of war or a widespread epidemic, then that person who in life read the Qur'ān the most should be buried first.

8. The task of placing the dead person in the grave must be carried out by men only. The deceased's male relatives are actually expected to place him or her in the grave.

9. It is not proper to hire others to wash, shroud or inter the deceased. It is expected that the person's relatives and family do these things. Islam attaches great importance to strong relations between family members in life and at death.

10. The deceased is placed in the grave on his right side with his face towards the *qiblah*.

11. Whoever places the dead in the grave should say: *Bismillāh wa 'alā millati rasūlillāh* (In the name of God, by God's grace, and following the *Sunnah* of the Prophet). The corpse is lowered into the grave from the rear of the grave.

12. Standing up in the cemetery until the body is put into the grave is not required. Except for those who place the deceased in the grave, the mourners may be seated.

13. It is recommended that those standing around the grave, after the corpse has been lowered into it and before the covering has been placed over it, throw three handfuls of earth into the grave.

14. It is an innovation to admonish the dead person after his death. Admonishing should be done during his dying.

15. It is recommended to pray for the dead person.

After the Burial

1. If the person died in debt it is the responsibility of his relatives to discharge the debt as soon as possible, provided that this is within their capacity.

2. The deceased's last wishes should be fulfilled except if they contradict the teachings of Islam; if, for example, he instructed his survivors to give an extra sum of money to one of his heirs, as Islam already regulates the inheritance for this group of people.

Condolences

1. It is a Muslim's duty to offer condolences, comfort, and sympathy to the bereaved. To do so contributes to strengthening relationships within Muslim society. Therefore, mixing socially with the bereaved family for a period following the death is Islamic conduct, helping to get them back to normal life as quickly as possible.

2. When offering condolences one's words should be chosen carefully. The right words should be used to convey sympathy and to encourage the bereaved to accept God's will.

3. Islamic phrases of sympathy are, for instance: *Ghafarallāhu limayyitikum* (May God forgive the deceased his sins) and *Innā lillāhi mā akhadha wa lahū mā a'ṭā wa Kullu shay'in 'indahū ilā ajalin musammā* (What God has taken or given does indeed belong to Him and He has an appointed time for every thing).

4. Comforting and encouraging the bereaved is required for as long as the necessity remains. Thus, the bereaved should be visited from time to time.

5. The bereaved family is not supposed to cook food for or serve visitors. On the contrary, friends, neighbours and relatives are advised to prepare food for them, for the loss of their loved one occupies the family's whole attention.

6. Showing sympathy to the bereaved is good conduct, but it should be done without exaggeration. Speeches

should be kept short and light; jokes, laughing and anything that may give offence should be avoided.

7. All innovative practices following the death of a Muslim (such as holding a 'wake' on the fortieth day, etc.) must be avoided.

Mourning

1. Though mourning over the dead is allowed in Islam, great differences exist between the Islamic viewpoint on this and the practice of Muslims at the present time.

2. Women have the right to mourn a deceased relative, for a period not exceeding three days. For widows the period of mourning may extend to four lunar months and ten days.

3. No loss, however great, should be permitted to sour one's outlook. Endurance should be shown by the bereaved, who are recommended to praise God and say: *Innā lillāhi wa-innā ilayhi rāji'ūn* (We belong to Him, to Him do we return).

4. Grief at the death of a relative or friend is normal. It is also normal and usual to see people weeping for the dead, and this is allowed in Islam. What is completely forbidden is to express grief by wailing, shrieking, beating the cheeks and tearing hair or clothes.

5. When mourning a dead person, care must be taken to avoid phrases that contradict Islamic principles, e.g. 'What will become of me now?' or 'Now our supporter is gone.' This implies relying on human beings rather than on Allah.

6. It is a Muslim's duty to advise those who wail for the dead in this way to stop doing so.

7. Islam prescribes that a widow may not remarry during

her period of mourning; it is considered impolite, therefore, to ask for a woman's hand during this period.

8. A widow in mourning may not wear clothes of saffron colour, or wear jewellery, or dye her hair with henna or use antimony on her eyes.

In this chapter we have confined ourselves to the most general and necessary rules of conduct for the burial. Those requiring more information should consult the various volumes of Islamic law.

18

Cemetery Architecture

Location

1. Locations distant from towns and villages are pointless for it makes the practice of visiting graves difficult.

2. Cemeteries should be reasonably close to towns. With expansion of towns they may eventually become a part of the town and may if necessary be made use of for further building, planting or other useful purposes, but only if the dead have decayed to soil. The principle to be kept in mind is that people should organize their affairs without harming the dead.

3. Cleanliness in Islam is required for the living and for the dead, so cemeteries should be kept clean.

Interior Grave Design

1. It is not desirable for anyone to have his own grave dug and prepared before he is dead, as some people do.

2. The grave must be dug deep and made spacious.

3. There are two ways of digging a grave, both of which are permissible, but the first is preferable. The first is to make a niche in the side of the grave facing the *qiblah*. The second is to excavate downwards in the middle of the grave.

Exterior Grave Design

1. Islam has a unique style in building graves and cemeteries that is characterized by humility, inextravagance and economy in costs and that avoids glorifying the dead in elaborate monuments.

2. The height of the grave should be only about a handspan above ground level. That serves to sufficiently distinguish the grave for it to be recognized as such and maintained.

3. Graves should not be raised above dug soil that remains after burying.

4. No form of construction should be erected on graves. If, however, having the graves clayed to maintain and keep them raised to within permissible bounds, so that wind or rain cannot damage them, that undoubtedly is permissible because it realizes a permissible objective. Exceeding the bounds of the permissible and/or any intent to decorate or other such vanities, are not allowed.

5. Upright tombstones on the grave itself are forbidden.

6. Graves must not be plastered with gypsum, paint or such like decoration, which are wholly inappropriate for a dead body decaying to soil.

7. Writing is not to be made on graves except for the name of the dead and that only for identification purposes and not for decoration.

19

Travelling

Travelling is not easy, but rather tiring and often complicated. Thus, Islam enjoins certain rules for travel to make it as light and enjoyable as possible:

1. When intending to travel, a Muslim should say two *rak'ahs* (*istikhāra* prayer), if possible, and seek proper guidance from God.

2. Certain superstitious beliefs and practices, observed by some people when a relative travels (such as refraining from cleaning the house immediately after the person's departure lest that might harm him) are completely forbidden, as Islam rejects all kinds of superstitions.

3. A Muslim should not refrain from travelling when he thinks he has seen a sign or omen against it.

4. It is better to take a companion when travelling, and to avoid travelling alone.

5. It is better to start a journey at the beginning of the day. And, if possible, to set out on a Thursday.

6. It is permissible to start a journey on any day and at any hour. The idea that one should not travel on Fridays is not in accordance with the teachings of Islam.

7. The ideal company while travelling consists of four people.

8. When getting in or on his conveyance, a Muslim is recommended to mention this phrase: *Subhānal-ladhī sakhkhara lanā hādhā wa mā kunnā lahū muqrinīn wa innā ilā Rabbinā la munqalibūn* (Glorified be He Who has subdued this to us, and we were not capable of subduing it. And to our Lord, surely, we are returning).

9. On bidding farewell, a Muslim should say, while shaking hands with the traveller: *Astawda' Allāh dīnaka wa amānataka wa Khawātima a'mālika* (May God preserve your faith, religious duties and conclusion of your deeds).

10. If a group of three or more are travelling together, one should be chosen as the leader, to organize the trip.

11. All those taking part in a journey should listen to and obey the leader. Disobedience to him and disagreeing with him could lead to arguments with undesirable consequences for all.

12. If a Muslim has more than one wife, then the only way to decide which wife accompanies him on a journey is to let them draw lots.

13. The same rule, as 12 above, should be observed when leaving to perform *ḥajj* or *'umrah*.

14. It is not advisable for a Muslim to take with him the Qur'ān or portions of it if he is travelling to countries which might dishonour it.

15. Women are not allowed to travel long distances unless accompanied either by *maḥrams* or their husbands.

16. To be polite, kind, helpful and co-operative to travelling companions is recommended. As is being solicitous to serve others and not allowing them to do everything.

17. It is the duty of a traveller in company to look after any member of the group who falls ill.

18. The expectation that those who travel to other countries should, upon their return, bring presents for relatives or friends makes travelling more difficult and more expensive.

19. If the journey is a long one, then the traveller is advised not to exert himself, but to take a rest whenever necessary.

20. If stopping for any reason, then it is a traveller's duty not to park his vehicle on the road or occupy a part of the road, for such action could hinder traffic and might also endanger his life and the lives of others.

21. When stopping or sleeping outdoors, the traveller should avoid places where there could be harmful creatures, especially at night.

22. When travellers stop, to take a rest or for any other reason, they should not divide themselves into groups or separate from one another, but rather gather in one group.

23. It is the duty of a Muslim traveller, to help those whom he meets who are in need of his help, by providing them with water or fuel, by repairing their vehicle, giving them a lift, or any other kind of possible assistance, irrespective of the religion, race or nationality of the person needing help.

24. Fasting during Ramaḍān while on a journey is allowed. If a Muslim feels able to fast while travelling he is allowed to do so, if not, he is allowed to break it.

25. For the ease of the traveller, it is permitted that he combines the noon and the afternoon prayers, and also the sunset and the evening prayers.

26. While on a journey, a Muslim may pray from his vehicle or astride his riding animal, in whatever direction he is travelling.

27. Prayers consisting of four *rak'ahs* are shortened to two *rak'ahs* on a journey.

28. The traveller is recommended to take advantage of the night hours for travelling.

29. It is recommended that a Muslim returns home as soon as the purpose of his travel is accomplished, especially after *ḥajj*.

30. When returning from a journey, arriving home at night should be avoided.

31. The first thing that a Muslim should do on returning to his home town is to go to the local mosque and pray two *rak'ahs*.

32. It is recommended to greet the traveller on his return with an embrace. A man may embrace another man, a woman another woman.

33. When about to enter a village, town or residential area, a traveller should pray by saying: *A'ūdhu bi kalimāt Allāh al-tāmmāt min sharri mā khalaq* (I seek refuge with the perfect words of Allah from the evil of what He has created).

34. Praying while travelling is recommended. In fact, the supplications (*du'ā'*) of a traveller are of special importance. Prayer here does not refer to the five obligatory daily prayers (*ṣalāt*), rather to spontaneous remembrance of God, asking Him for perfection, guidance, and help.

35. Saying *Allāhu Akbar* (God is great) as he climbs an ascent, and *Subḥān Allāh* as he makes the descent, are recommended of a Muslim when travelling.

36. Among the good manners expected of a traveller is to overlook and forget his companions' mistakes, chat with them kindly, share food and drink with them, and avoid disputes.

37. When travelling on a riding animal and passing through an area where there is grass and water, the traveller should proceed slowly; when passing through a barren or desert area, he should proceed quickly.

38. It is not recommended for Muslims to go to non-Islamic lands and live there permanently. If a Muslim travels to a non-Islamic country there should be a good reason.

20

Sports

1. To become addicted to watching sports amounts to a waste of time and has hardly any benefit for a Muslim. In Islam, sports are encouraged insofar as they are a means to build strong, healthy bodies. Sport must be treated as a means and not as an end; when sport becomes an end in itself it is prohibited. This does not apply to the case of physical education instructors, or trainers.

2. Sports dress should be designed and made in accordance with the rules of Islamic dress discussed above.

3. Placing or accepting a wager by contestants on the result of a race or other event is forbidden except in a camel, horse or elephant race. For non-contestants, betting and gambling of any sort is forbidden.

4. All kinds of sports which endanger life, as in modern wrestling or boxing, are forbidden.

5. All forms of sports which harm any animal, such as oxen, cocks, etc. are forbidden, for this contradicts the humanitarian demands of Islam.

6. The most highly recommended types of sports in Islam are those involving some sort of projectile, such as shooting or throwing.

21

Treatment of Animals

1. Mercy and kindness should characterize all aspects of the treatment of animals.

2. Animals should carry loads according to their strength and capability.

3. Slaughtering animals should be carried out skilfully and perfectly, so that an animal is not tortured in the process.

4. As mentioned in the rules of travelling, when passing with a beast through an area where there is grass and water, a traveller should proceed slowly. When, on the other hand, he is passing through a barren, or desert area, he should proceed quickly.

5. Killing non-useful but nevertheless unharmful animals or insects, such as moths or small birds, should be avoided.

6. Slaughtering animals who produce milk, eggs, etc. should be postponed for as long as possible.

7. Castrating (emasculating) animals or spaying the female is forbidden in Islam.

8. Killing some types of creatures should be avoided, unless they become harmful, such as bees, ants, hoopoes and frogs.

9. One should not hesitate to kill the following four types of creatures: scorpions, mice, snakes and geckos.

10. To refrain from killing snakes out of superstition indicates a weak faith.

11. To cross a horse and a donkey in order to produce a mule should be avoided.

12. To use gold or silver in an animal's saddle or bridle, or in a dog's line, or to bedeck an animal with silk, is forbidden, for it is a waste of money and betrays arrogance and pride.

13. To brand an animal on the face is forbidden. Branding an animal on any other part of its body is allowed, provided no harm is done to it, and branding is confined to necessary limits.

14. When beating an animal, striking its face must be avoided.

15. To set animals against each other, such as cocks, oxen or sheep, for the sake of fun or for any other reason, is completely forbidden in Islam and considered an act of cruelty.

16. It is not allowed to sell or buy an animal which is still in need of its mother. If such a transaction has already been carried out, it must be annulled.

17. When hunting birds or animals, hunting young animals still in need of their mothers should be avoided; likewise killing a mother who has young ones should be avoided, as the young ones would then die.

18. Hunting animals during *ḥajj* or *'umrah* is forbidden. If it should happen that a Muslim does hunt or kill an animal or bird while performing *ḥajj* or *'umrah*, then it is his duty to make special atonement.

19. Animals which feed on filth should be avoided for meat and for riding. Neither should their milk be used until the animals have been confined to clean fodder for a sufficient period.

20. If a Muslim owns livestock, birds or animals, then it is his responsibility before God to feed them and to take care of them.

21. Using an animal as a target for shooting practise with a gun or bow is forbidden.

22. To seek refuge in God from the devil whenever one hears a donkey braying is a recommended act.

23. A Muslim should ask God to bless him whenever he hears a rooster crow.

24. Every animal is created for a certain purpose such as milking, riding, etc. Therefore, animals should be used according to their purpose.

25. Dismembering a dead animal is forbidden.

26. One should never curse an animal.

27. Animals are of two kinds, clean and unclean. Unclean animals are dogs and pigs. When a dog drinks out of a vessel, it must be washed seven times, using earth once.

28. A dog may not be owned by a Muslim except for two reasons: (a) as a watch-dog; (b) as a hunting dog. The place for such dogs, however, is outside the house, not inside.

Bibliography

The Holy Qur'ān, translated by M. M. Pickthall (New York, 1977).
Al-Albānī, Nāsir al-Dīn, *Ādāb al-Zafāf* (Beirut, 1977), *Manāsik al-Hajj wa al-'Umrah* (Beirut, 1979), *Mukhtasar Saḥīh al-Bukhārī* (Beirut, 1981), *Hijāb al-Mar'a al-Muslima fī al-Kitāb wa al-Sunnah* (Beirut, 1979).
Al-Ghazālī, *Al-ādāb fī al-dīn* (Beirut, 1980).
Hamidullah, Muhammad, *Introduction to Islam* (Damascus, 1977).
Ibn Qayyim al-Jawziyyah, *Tuhfat al-Maulūd* (Damascus, 1971).
Murdock, G. P., *Social Structure* (New York, 1949).
Al-Nawawī, *Al-Nawawī's Forty Ḥadīth* (Damascus, 1979); *Al-Adhkār* (Damascus, 1971).
Qutb, Sayyid, *Milestones* (I.I.F.S.O., 1977).
Qutb, Muhammad, *Islam the Misunderstood Religion* (Damascus, 1977).
Sakr, A. H., *Pork: Possible Reasons for its Prohibition* (published by the author, 1975).
Sumner, W. G., *Folkways* (New York, 1965).
Tabrīzī, Al-Khatīb, *Mishkāt al-Maṣābīḥ*, English translation by James Robson (Lahore, 1981).
Vanderbilt, Amy, *The World Book Encyclopaedia* (Chicago, 1972).
Academic American Encyclopedia (Danbury, 1982).
Encyclopedia Americana (Danbury, 1979).
Encyclopaedia Britannica (London, 1971).
Encyclopaedia of Islam (London, 1960).
Encyclopedia of Social Science (London, 1962).

Index

Ablution, 31, 108, 176–7; removal of impurities, 65–7
Ādāb al-Islām, 13–14, 16–25, 28, 31 35–6, 38–40, 42, 44–9, 53
Adhān, 127
Adornment, for men, 68–9; beard, 69, 109; hair, 68; moustache, 69, 109; perfume, 69; signet ring, 69
Adornment, for women, 68, 70; clothes, 82–3, 85, 182; face and hands, 70–1, 118, 182; hair, 70–1, 182; perfume, 71
Adultery, 42; penalties for, 42
Al-'amāl al-Ṣāliḥ, 18
Alcohol, 33, 42, 48, 73, 77, 124; prohibition of, 33, 42, 73, 77, 124; restrictions, 47
Animals: considered impure, 65, 73; considered pests, 46, 193; hunting, 194; sacrifice of, 28, 97, 115, 129, 149; slaughter of, 28–9, 32, 65, 113, 115, 128–9, 147, 193–5; treatment of, 193–5
Apostasy, 42; penalties for, 42
Aqīqah, 97
Architecture, 87

Bathing, 41, 65–6, 109; after lovemaking, 122; after menstruation and child-bed, 66; before congregational prayer, 66, 109; method of, 66–7; obligatory, 66; rules of, 66–7
Bed, 19, 45, 57; design and construction, 57; height, 19, 57; position, 58
Belief, 48; freedom of, 48
Bereavement, 30, 175, 180–1
Bid'ah, 29–30

Births, 26, 127–8, 166; announcement of, 127
Biryānī, 47
Bride, 37
Bridegroom, 37
Burial, 175, 177–9, 182; time for, 178
Business transactions, 146, 164

Celebrations, 164–6
Cemetery, 29, 171–2, 177–9, 183; architecture, 183; location, 183; visiting, 29, 171–2
Child-bed, 62, 123
Childbirth, 15, 31, 62
Children, 12, 23, 33, 39, 51, 77, 95–8, 100, 109, 114, 118, 127–8, 166, 168; conduct of, 39, 77, 99–100, 168, 170; conduct towards parents, 99–102; education of, 97–8; naming, 127, 131–2; new-born, 128, 131; shaving the head, 129
Christianity, 47, 49
Circumcision, 33, 129–30; conditions for, 129–30
Cleanliness: of clothes, 51, 65, 82, 108–9, 136, 161, 169; of dwelling, 88–9; of mosque, 27, 108–9, 169; personal, 27, 31–21, 51, 65–8, 70–1, 77–9, 108–9, 123, 136, 161; when eating, 73–5, 77–9
Clothes, 22, 25, 32, 35, 41, 51, 65, 82–4, 169, 182
Condolences, 180
Corruption, 18
Cosmetics, 41
Cremation, 16, 178

Daughters, treatment of, 42, 97
Day of Resurrection, 45
Death-bed, 16
Debt, discharge of, 39, 179
Diet, 16, 32, 47–8; non-Muslims, 48; restrictions, 47
Dhu'l-Hijja, 113
Disease(s), 21, 31–3, 65; protection against, 65
Divorce, 31, 43, 96, 118, 146; discouragement of, 31; right of, 42; rules of, 48
Dog(s), 34, 79, 88, 195; diseases from, 34, 79, 195
Dowry, 120
Dreams and nightmares, 59
Dress, 16, 22, 40, 44, 47–9, 53, 81–5, 113, 164, 191; moderation in, 35, 40–1, 44, 47, 53, 81; on medical grounds, 83; prohibitions, 81, 83–4; sports, 191
Drinking, 17, 23, 31–2, 36, 46, 52, 60, 77–9, 108, 156, 159, 188; forbidden, 77, 159; moderation in, 35; vessels, 77–9, 89, 195
Dwelling place, 87–9; cleanliness of, 88–9; safety of, 89
Du'ā', 112, 162, 188

Eating, 19, 21, 23, 25, 31–2, 45, 48, 52, 60, 74–5, 77, 108, 157, 174; as a family, 75; moderation in, 32, 35, 76, 157; non-Muslims, 48, 74
Education, 97–8
Etiquette, 17, 19–20, 74; Western, 19, 74

Family, 36–7, 39, 77, 91–2, 114; life, 39, 92; name, 43; problems, 95; rules of conduct, 91–2
Fasting, 15, 18, 34, 44, 62, 111, 113, 116–17, 123, 146, 156, 158, 187; exemption from, 34; when travelling, 15, 187
Feast(s), 26, 63, 113; *Aḍḥā*, 27, 113–15; *Fiṭr*, 27, 113–14; meal, 113; observation of, 113; prayers, 113–16
Festivals, 18, 47
Food, 16–17, 21, 35, 47, 50, 73–7, 156, 159, 166, 188; *biryānī*, 47; forbidden, 50, 73–4, 159; in moderation, 73, 76; lawful, 73, 77; not recommended, 76; preparation of, 73; wastage of, 35, 76

Gift(s), 21–2, 27, 138, 167–8
God, *passim*
Gold, 35, 69, 77, 88, 194
Grandparents, 168
Grave(s), 22, 30, 38, 171, 179, 183; decoration, 171, 184; design, 183–4
Greetings, 47, 150–2, 161, 173
Guardian, 43, 119
Guest(s), 26, 36, 155–8, 162; hospitality toward, 36, 155–8

Ḥajj, 18, 27, 121, 186, 188, 194
Ḥalāl, 47
Ḥarām, 47
Heirs, 16, 180
Hereafter, 20, 171
Hijrah, 30
Hospital(s), 159–60; patients, 160
Host, 26, 154–6, 158–9; duties of, 154–6, 158–9
Housing, 21–2, 36, 87–8
Husband, 21, 37–9, 41, 43–4, 65, 70, 91, 93, 119, 122, 125, 154, 163; conduct, 122–3; property, 96

Imām, 110–12, 114, 171
Immorality, 18
Impurities, 65, 67; removal of, 66–7
Inheritance, 16, 180; share of, 16
Invitation(s), 27, 136, 159; to a meal, 26, 157–9, to a wedding, 26, 136
Islam, *passim*; broad objectives, 14; emergence of, 13; goals of, 18, 20; historical, 10; normative, 10, 18, 29; principles of, 30, 49; unity of, 29, 46
Islamic: behaviour, 24, 137–44, 156, 166, 173; calendar, 49; community, 12, 14, 17, 21, 47, 114, 135, 172; culture, 46–7, 114; customs, 14, 16, 49; law(s), 18, 32, 42, 50, 93, 114, 117, 183; manners, 12, 13–17, 20, 26, 29–30, 39, 44, 46–7, 51, 137, 156, 158, 173; teachings, 15–16, 20, 42–3, 52, 60, 81, 98, 155, 171–2, 180, 185; way of life, 14–16, 18, 35, 47, 49

Joking, 148; avoidance of, 148, 180

Ka'bah, 29, 62–3, 115, 145; circumambulation of, 62–3
Khuṭbah, 110–12, 114

Laughter, 23, 147; avoidance of, 147, 180

198

Lavatory, 60–2, 108; correct use of, 60–2; outdoors, 61–2; purification after use, 60
Law: family, 48; Islamic, 18; personal, 48
Love-making, 24, 123, 125; moderation in, 123

Mahram, 41, 44, 117–18, 154, 163, 186
Marriage, 19, 36–7, 40, 43, 48, 91, 93, 117–20; celebrations, 121; contract, 38, 93, 120; decision, 43, 119; dowry, 120; fasting, 123; lasting, 38, 120; preparatory steps, 38; proposal, 42, 118–19; role of wife, 94, 123; rules of, 48, 93; temporary, 38, 120
Maulid, 30
Meat: *halāl*, 47, 73; *harām*, 28, 32, 47, 65, 73
Menstruation, 15, 31, 34, 43, 62–3, 103, 114, 122–3, 170; fasting during, 62; husband's conduct during, 122; praying during, 62; prohibitions during, 62–3, 103, 122, 170; psychological effect, 31, 34
Minbar, 108, 110, 112
Mi'rāj, 30
Miswāk, 59, 68
Money, 35–6, 52, 180; constraints on spending, 35–6
Mosque(s), 25, 27, 36, 62–3, 92, 107–10, 113, 161, 169–70, 177, 188; conduct in, 108, 110–12, 114, 169–70; design, 107
Mourning, 39, 181; period of, 39
Murder, 42

Nadhr, 146
Names: forbidden, 132; recommended, 131–2
Neighbours, 166–7, 180

Oath(s), 145–6
Orphan, 119

Parents, 23, 39, 96–100, 131, 166, 168; conduct towards children, 96–8, 131–2
Parent-child relationships, 39, 99–101, 166
Pilgrimage, 18, 27, 62, 113, 121, 125, 176
Polygamy, 124

Polytheism, 28
Prayer(s), 15, 27, 29–31, 34, 36, 44–5, 49–50, 57, 62, 66, 75, 92, 98, 109–12, 116, 122, 127, 145, 155, 170–1, 187–8; ablution before, 31, 66, 109; *'asr*, 57; call to, 127; congregational, 27, 30, 36, 66, 109–12, 170–1; exemption from, 34; *fajr*, 14, 49, 59; funeral, 176–7; *'ishā'*, 49, 57, 154, 162; when travelling, 187–8; *zuhr*, 57
Property, 42, 48, 94, 96, 117
Prophet Muhammad, 14, 18, 23–4, 29, 38–9, 43–4, 47, 50, 59, 68, 99, 104, 108, 110–11, 127, 145, 160, 162, 165–6, 170
Puberty, 51, 97
Punishment, 42

Qiblah, 29, 61, 179, 183
Qur'ān, 12, 14–15, 20, 30, 35, 37, 46–7, 50, 60, 63, 97, 103, 108, 111, 145, 165, 170, 177–8, 186

Ramaḍān, 15, 18, 44, 62, 113, 116, 123, 187
Relations, 39, 165, 177, 179, 181
Roads, behaviour on, 172–4

Sacrifice, 28, 97, 115–16, 129
Sārī, 47
Seminal defilement, 63, 103; prohibition during, 63, 103, 170
Sex, 40; benefits of, 40–1; illicit, 18
Sexes: mixing of, 114, 124, 155, 164, 173; separation of, 41, 164
Sexual behaviour, 40; control of, 40; privacy in, 41
Sexual intercourse, 31, 34, 43, 62–3, 117, 122–3; during menses, 34, 62, 122
Shaking hands, 148–9, 186
Sharī'ah, 28, 38
Shuhadā', 178
Sickness, 159–60, 166
Siesta, 57, 154; between prayers, 57
Silver, 35, 88, 194; ring, 69; vessels, 77
Singing, 37
Slaughter of animals, 28–9, 32, 193
Sleeping, 57–8; after eating, 76; after love-making, 122; awakening from, 59; praying before, 58; preparation for, 57–8
Sneezing, 33, 55–6
Sports, 191

Sunnah, 12, 14–15, 20, 30, 46, 50, 97, 124
Superstitions, 185
Swearing, 145–6

Table manners, 73–9, 158–9
Tableware, 73, 76
Taḥnīk, 127
Talking, 25 141
Tawḥīd, 28
Transactions, financial, 42, 146, 164
Travelling, 15, 18, 24, 46, 89, 111, 125, 173, 185, 188–9, 193; assistance to fellow travellers, 187; choosing a leader, 186; conduct toward fellow travellers, 188; fasting, 187

'Ulamā', 82
'Umrah, 121, 125, 176, 186, 194

Virgin, 118–19, 124
Visitors, 153–5, 160, 180
Vows, 29, 146–7; null and void, 29

Walīmah, 124
Walking, 52, 174, 177
Wedding(s), 16, 26, 36, 121, 166; feast, 37, 123–4, 158

Weeping, 147, 181
Widow, 39, 181–2; period of mourning, 39, 181–2
Wife, 37–9, 41, 43, 91–6, 124–5; accompanying husband on a journey, 186; conduct of, 94–6, 118; conduct toward, 91–3; 125; deceased, 38; fasting, 94; infertile, 118; property, 95, 118; role in marriage, 94–5, 122; search for, 117
Women: after menstruation, 63; conduct outside the house, 163; divorced, 118; during menstruation and child-bed, 62–3, 103, 114, 123, 170; guardian, 119–20; make-up and adornment, 70; protection of, 40–2
Worship, 48, 110–12, 169–70, 172; freedom of, 48
Wuḍū', 31, 57, 59, 109–10, 122; before going to bed, 57; between intercourse, 122; invalidation of, 110; on awakening, 59

Yawning, 56

Zakāt, 116